By the author of:

The Star-Borne:
  A Remembrance for the Awakened Ones

The Legend of Altazar:
  A Fragment of the True History of Planet Earth

Invoking Your Celestial Guardians

Yet to be published:

11:11 – The Journey through the Doorway

Temple Invisible

Part Two of the 11:11 Trilogy:
  The Council of One

Part Three of the 11:11 Trilogy:
  Beyond the Beyond

EL·AN·RA

The Healing of Orion

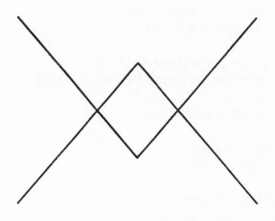

SOLARA

STAR-BORNE UNLIMITED

Star-Borne Unlimited
2005 Commonwealth Drive
Charlottesville, VA 22901

First Edition published July 1991
Second Edition published October 1991

ISBN # 1-878246-04-6

Cover painting by:
Geoffrey Chandler

Interior Illustrations:
Siolana/Raney Alexander

Book Design by:
Solara & Elara Zacandra

Typesetting by:
Elara Zacandra

Printed in the United States of America.

This book
is lovingly dedicated
to the One . . .

and to those
who choose
to step forward
courageously
into the Unknown,

making visible the Invisible.

INTRODUCTION.........................

The story of EL*AN*RA first appeared as a fragment which I wrote a few years ago. It was simply one of several unrelated fragments which I felt inspired to write. I definitely had no intention of turning it into a book. When it began to expand into several chapters, I was most surprised. I soon realized that my next step would be to fully explore the realms of our *off planet* memories, especially those concerning the great conflicts of duality inherent in Orion. *(Off planet memories are those which pertain to our experiences on other star systems.)*

Throughout this time, I have had repeated interactions with those who are still enacting the Orion patterning, beginning to recognize the presence of Orion implants in some of the ones whom I encountered. Finally, I understood the tremendous importance for all of us to retrieve our memories of our Orion experiences that they may be cleared and fully understood. And that this step would be necessary so we could graduate from this dimensional universe.

Once again like my earlier book, *The Legend of Altazar*, this is a simple story, plainly written. It contains humor, pathos and courage. But please do not let yourself be fooled by its simplicity. The lessons of this book are extremely powerful and timely for all of us. If you begin this story, please commit yourself to finish it, for the journey is well worth your time. The story of EL*AN*RA contains the keys to freedom, which is why I had to write it. And I now lovingly pass it on to you.

Please know that this book has been placed into your hands because you, yourself, have called it forth to be. You are now ready to remember and complete another level of our long forgotten history. The story of EL*AN*RA is written for each of us. We have all been playing out the great cosmic drama of duality for countless aeons. For most of that lengthy span, we have accepted that duality and separation were our predominant reality, so immersed in the waters of oblivion had we become.

In order for us now to move forward and graduate into new levels of mastery and freedom, we must first turn our attention to healing all polarities, reuniting the fragments of our multi-dimensional beings, thus bringing them back into conscious Oneness.

And you might ask what this has to do with the constellation of Orion? Orion is of vast importance in our sacred quest for full remembrance since it is the master template of duality for this entire dimensional universe. The three stars in the belt of Orion, what we call the EL*AN*RA *(Mintaka, Al Nilam, Al Nitak in traditional astronomy)*, are the main control points or pins which hold our dimensional universe into position. It is through the central star in Orion's belt which is the Eye of AN that we shall travel as we make our long awaited journey through the Doorway of the 11:11.

This book is lovingly offered to you that you may make your final preparations in order to become ready for the next step on our homeward journey. For we shall not be able to move through the Doorway of the 11:11 until the healing of Orion has been achieved, both internally and externally.

Orion is divided into three zones. The upper zone is under the leadership of the star Betelgeuse. Here are located the Councils of Light and the Lords of Light. The lower zone is controlled by the star Rigel and is the home of the Dark Lords ruled by the Triad known as the OMNI. In the central portion of Orion is a zone of overlap which contains the EL*AN*RA. The EL*AN*RA could be referred to as the Great Light for it signifies the sacred alchemical union of dark and light into One. It is served by Lord Metatron and the Council of the Elohim.

Throughout our cycle of service in this dimensional universe we have been subject to the laws of duality as embodied by Orion. As actors in the great cosmic play of duality, all of us have donned both the dark robes and the white robes repeatedly, endlessly, each time believing that the designated role we had chosen to act out was our only reality.

This cycle of duality will continue on forever until we can achieve true completion. The opportunity for mastery of the illusions of duality and separation is now at hand. It is time for us to finally remove all our robes, both light and dark, to let go of our illusions that we are right and others are wrong, that we are separate entities – and to see that under all the layers of disguise, *everyone wears a body of Light!* Thus shall we be ready to rise into the full knowing that each of us are fragments of the One.

This inherent Oneness is the lesson of the EL*AN*RA. Orion itself, is like a large Antarion Conversion. Within its zone of overlap, all dualities have merged into One. Our present challenge is for each of us to create that zone of overlap within ourselves until we are firmly, irrevocably, anchored into Oneness. We become free, because we are no longer affected by the twists and turns, ups and downs of duality.

We have become mirrored reflections of the One. That in turn frees us further, for we have hereby loosened our alignment with our present Great Central Sun System. We have graduated from our spiral of evolution within this dimensional universe and are ready to move through the Doorway of the 11:11 onto a new spiral. This new spiral contains a patterning of octaves and is aligned with an even Greater Central Sun System.

Each of our beings is like a strand of light. As we evolve and reawaken, our threads of light begin to vibrate with a more highly calibrated frequency. This refinement of resonance draws us ever closer together with the others who have also chosen to reawaken and remember. As we step into and embody our inherent Oneness, our strands of light begin to weave themselves together into the fabric of the Greater Reality.

Between this present moment and the end of the year 2011, there shall be a mammoth, irrevocable separation taking place upon planet Earth. That is why we are in such a deeply critical time. This shall be known as the final separation. What is splitting apart are the portions of humanity who choose to remain anchored in duality and those who now know that we are One. This separation shall come about in a gradual manner, although its movement away from the other shall be increasingly accelerated.

The ones who have chosen Oneness and who are reweaving themselves together shall become increasingly transparent, for they are transforming into true beings of light. Their silicon bodies are already in the process of formation.

At the appointed moment of the final separation, our planet Earth shall shed her skin. This will take place gently in the merest of instants, possibly while you are asleep. You can visualize this as peeling the skin of an apple with a knife in one smooth, circular movement. The discarded outer shell of Earth shall be blown through the sky to its appointed destination, a parallel planet which has already been prepared to serve this purpose. Earth's skin shall wrap itself around this new planet; then those who have chosen to remain in duality will begin to awaken, only to discover that nothing has changed, they are still where they were before.

Yet, they shall soon discover that some of us are missing. But right after this initial discovery, we will begin to quickly fade from their misty memories like a rapidly dissolving sunset. Life will continue on as always on the playing fields of duality. New York City will still be noisily teeming with life. Cars shall drive people to work. Birth, death, struggle, passion, fear, trying, illusion – the same old cycle endlessly repeating itself, enlivened this time by the additional experience of Armageddon. It is duality in anguish from the pain of separation, attempting to vanquish the other half of itself.

And what shall happen to those of us who choose Oneness, who have woven ourselves together into the fabric of the Greater Reality? When the mighty wind of the dragons blows all else away, we will remain in our Islands of Light. So shall the central core of the Earth. After she sheds her skin, Earth's inner layers of mountains and valleys shall be revealed in all their pristine purity. And we will have hereby passed through the Doorway of the 11:11. We are ready to build on the new.

Maybe now you realize how very important and long lasting are the results of the choices you are now facing. Each of us must choose which reality we are going to live in. Shall you choose to remain in duality or will you choose Oneness? Please make this choice with your full conscious awareness! Never before have we been so needed for the fulfillment of the Divine Plan on Earth.

So in full acknowledgement of your inherent magnificence, with deep gratitude for your perseverance, commitment and courage, I present to you the next step on our great adventure towards full remembrance and freedom!

Solara Antara Amaa-Ra

I am one of the early ones . . .
now weary of body,
deep aching of soul.
We are easy to recognize.

What secret sadness do we carry?
The profound well of sorrow
that the very fabric of our beings
has been immersed in
for aeons beyond measure.

Is not our penance
this endless earthly span
that we, ourselves, chose to do
back so very long ago
that the memory has dimmed.

Now we walk our final miles
upon this planet earth
with loving dedication
and strength of will,
forcing our ancient, weary forms
to take yet another step
    and another . . .
            and another . . .

For this long road
we must complete
ere we finally depart
to fly freely once again
returning to Heart's Source,
Beyond the Beyond.

TABLE OF CONTENTS

A Fragment of Remembrance . .

The woman sat silently on the roof swaddled in a pale yellow cloth. Above her spread the vast canopy of stars. So many stars there were, keeping watch on endless worlds within worlds . . .

Then came that overwhelming feeling . . . a deep emotion of forgetting . . . forgetting something of immense importance. This sensation had been reoccurring frequently during the past several months. It filled her with a profound longing to know, to remember, what apparently had been forgotten. This perplexed her, for she knew not what was expected of her, only that it was of utmost importance to remember. But what?

As she sat lost in silent contemplation, a brilliant star caught her attention. Yes, this was the same star which had flickered and beamed at her for weeks. Why out of all the countless stars above, did this one particular star keep catching her attention? It was as if this star was calling out to her, radiating its energy, forcing her to recognize and acknowledge its presence.

Suddenly a tunnel opened up and she knew that she could travel through this doorway all the way to her star. Pushing back shreds of her fear of the Unknown, the woman allowed herself to be drawn into it. Maybe this mysterious star would hold some clues to what she needed so desperately to remember.

Arriving at the distant star, she saw spheres, numerous round orbs connected by tubes or passageways. Quickly, the woman pulled herself back into the body which she had left sitting on the roof, somehow sensing that what she was about to experience should not be rushed.

A strong wind came up suddenly, then died away . . .

She wanted so much to remember, yet knew that when she did, nothing in her life would remain unchanged.

ORION

Heavenly watchman
ever on duty.
Celestial sentinel
protecting three points.
Gateway Guardian,
Protector of the Unknown.

ORION
controversial
abode of light & dark,
united in sacred task
guarding control points
pinning dimensional universe
into predestined position.

As I enter your forcefield,
runway of sword lights up.
Hitherto unseen stars
illuminate my pathway
to the central door.

The Call is sounded:
EL*AN*RA . . .
I proceed upwards
as pulsating star path
reveals itself.

ORION . . .
some know you well
as a battleground,
a place where evil dwells.
You are but a warrior
assuming battle stance,

17

*simply to protect
the sacred doorway.*

*Drawing ever closer,
fear begins to rise.
Chilly currents of doubt
stir, yet stop me not.
Onward I proceed,
guided by Spirit's Call
to destination unknown
that lies beyond,
       beyond,
beyond all experience
remembered.*

*Deep within inner sanctum,
place of silent knowing,
memories awaken
that beyond this door
beckons a universe
so familiar and dear,
imbued with Essence of Home.*

*For countless aeons
have I carried
unspoken yearning
within my heart.
Now doubt and fears
must be set aside,
gathering together
all my fragments,
I focus and surrender
to the fateful journey
that has finally begun.*

Pulled magnetically
upon overpowering currents,
spiraling inward,
*   inward*
into penetrating darkness. . .
total absence of Light.

Shall I suffocate?
Shall I cease to be?
Pulled deeper inside
into the absolute void
of purest nothingness.

Bits and pieces
are ripped away,
outworn garments
torn asunder
as I go under
into Sea of Oblivion,
deepest, darkest blackness.

It is peaceful here
floating as nothing
within nothing.
No yearnings, no thoughts,
no separate identity. . .
all encompassing darkness.

Through it all
I am ever drawn
magnetically, irrevocably,
deeper, deeper
into the center,
inside, inside,
always inside.

Finally, a glimmer of Light!
I stir, almost awakening,
wanting to reach for the Light,
but some dim memory warns me
not to venture forward.
I must remain
in the womb of the unborn,
in the stillness of the unmanifest
as long as I can.

For doubt it not,
the Light shall seek me out,
it shall come to me of its own,
signaling the beginning of birth.
The Light shall send me forth
through the opposite doorway
into realms of greater radiance
than can possibly be imagined.

The dawn of homecoming
arises in fullest splendor.
Radiant beings of Light
shall guide my way
through octaves of awareness
so long forgotten.

Gazing in quiet wonder upon
my newly created form of Light,
perceiving its transparency,
glowing rainbow tubes
of flowing liquid Light,
outstretched wings in flight.

Close though I may be,
it is not journey's end.
Directly ahead of me

a pulsating, rotating,
swirling spiral galaxy
shoots off cascades
of streaming gases,
a flaming spiral,
the power of raw energy
and it blocks my path!

Nowhere to escape.
Quickly entering its sphere,
I burn and dissolve
into a drop of Essence pure.
This drop becomes One
with fiery Central Sun
until it is gently released.

Once again, flying freely
through dimensional heavens,
overlapping in endless expanse,
heart space channel,
now the Call is heard,
the sound of breath.
It is the breath of my star,
the star of my being.
I return to the Zone of Home.

Beyond the Beyond.

Chapter One:
KURALA

Once upon a fragile filament of distant memory, this story was true. Now, it is not. You ask how that can be? It is because histories can be erased; in fact, they call to us to be erased. It is simply part of remembering and releasing. We remember in order to become complete. In the process of remembering, we find wholeness as we merge with hitherto forgotten fragments of ourselves. During this sacred merger, the sealed off memories are released, thus do we become ever lighter and freer as we retrace our footprints back home – erasing them gently behind us.

The story of Kurala is the story of my shame – how I too, appeared to fall. How I misused my Divinely given power so I could experience all facets of the human experience in order to develop compassionate understanding for all of humanity, wherever they might find themselves upon the spiral of evolution.

These experiences happened to me so long ago, that even I have almost forgotten the details, though I remember well the lessons and the pain. They have been indelibly seared into my soul, never to be forgotten until I had finally returned to full remembrance of my true state of being.

From the experience of Kurala, I learned irrevocably, to never again abuse power and authority over others. I also learned to fear my vast power. Since then, in a cycle of arduous atonement, I have often chosen to surround myself with domineering tyrants. Safely cocooned within the role of victim, I did not have to be challenged with either the power of my wisdom or the wisdom of my power. Here I have hidden throughout much of my cycle of earthly embodiments. You could often find me crouching in the corner, eyes open wide with terror, anguish twisting my heart. Crying enough tears to water the entire planet, lamenting my lot – and always too frightened of myself to become free.

Throughout the embodiments following my experience as Kurala, my sight remained surprisingly clear. I saw everything, deeply penetrating behind the disguises and veils of rampant illusion. The clarity of my vision continually unmasked and thus threatened those who lived by corruption and deceit. Often this served as my undoing; many times they killed me by torture or burning.

I was usually a willing sacrifice, welcoming my impending death with head held high. As one who could clearly see the Truth; I had taken on the role of the stalwart Witness. I simply observed and noted the many abuses which I encountered in silence, preferring to be killed *(sometimes eagerly offering myself)* rather than speaking my Truth and openly wielding my authority and power again.

"How does an Angel, a free flying being of Light, so deeply enmesh and imprison herself?" you ask. "How does she allow herself to become so small and diminished?"

Innumerable times have I asked myself the very same question. Until finally, the light of understanding dawned within me. While I shall claim Kurala's story as

my own, possibly you can see that it is your story as
well. Each of us carries a fragment of her within us.
Each of us has atoned for what we judged ourselves as
our fall from grace. Each of us is now becoming whole
and free . . .

So as an act of loving service to all of us incarnate
ones, I shall share my tale of shame for the final time.
Great indeed, is the effort required to remember what
has almost been totally erased, like reading invisible
ink in the penetrating darkness of a moonless night. So
thin and frail has this memory become . . .

I know that as I touch it, it shall turn into dust.
Finally, I will be complete with Kurala's history. . . . Free
to move to a New Octave on the Golden Spiral . . . . .

KURALA IMAGE GALAXITRON
Experiment Z104ZZL
Distortion Frequency: Δ6QB-000
Grid Lapse Null Zone

BLACK CUBE IN POSITION ::: VECTOR 6 :::
CREATED BY PHANTOM PHOTONS ::: ASTRAL
DENSITY PLANE G14 ::: CUBE ::: EMITTING :::
DISCORDANT ::: SONAR ::: PULSES ::: ON :::
SCHEDULE ::: ::: THE ::: SNARE ::: IS ::: SET :::
::: INVERSE ::: GRID ::: IS ::: PUT ::: INTO :::
POSITION ::: ::: THE ::: TRAP ::: AWAITS ::: ITS
::: CHOSEN ::: VICTIM ::: ::: FULL ::: ALERT ::: IN
::: BLACK ::: CUBE ::: NULL ::: ZONE ::: :::
WAITING ::: ::: :::

WIND ::: VORTEX ::: ACTIVATED ::: ::: WHIRL-
WINDS ::: OF ::: DUST ::: CREATING ::: CHAOS
::: AND ::: CONFUSION ::: ::: VISIBILITY ::: ZERO
::: ::: PARTICULATE ::: MATTER ::: COSMIC :::
DEBRIS ::: CHURNING ::: ::: DISCORDANT :::
DECIBELS ::: SHRIEK ::: ::: :::

Suddenly an angel appears.
  She is lost,
        cannot see her way through clouds of dust.

Grey particulate matter sticks to her wings,
        weighs them down.
  Flying becomes difficult.

The howling winds pelt her with increasing momentum.
  Her robes begin to shred.
        She cries a silent scream of fear.

Heavy wings drag her down.
  Falling, crying, falling, crying.
        Into the abyss of the null zone.

Grids interlock over her.
  The net is closed.
        Density crushes.
  Immense pain and terror.

Cannot get free.
  Her entire being screaming pain.
        Confusion reigns.
  Darkness prevails.

  She is trapped . . .

The palace was enormous, all darkened plum and lime green, and revoltingly shiny. So shiny, that it appeared to be constantly wet. The walls themselves were slick and slippery. Curved, pointed spires, each of them different, protruded at weird angles in numerous directions. Nothing contained the slightest hint of symmetry, balance or harmony. The air was stale and moist. The smell of it was overly fragrant, like rotting orchids. To this place Kurala was taken. This was to be her prison.

She lay on the floor in a frightened heap, too scared to even cry. Occasionally large black spider people walked by and poked at her with one of their many hairy, black legs. Kurala pretended to be dead; in fact, she wished herself to be. Everything about this terrible place assaulted her being. Her sense of purity of self couldn't bear it. The very air screamed foulness to her. What a travesty and degradation! How could such a place exist in God's creation?

In her behalf, we shall state that poor Kurala tried to hold on for as long as she could. However, there came a time when she could no longer withstand the assault. She gave up and allowed her being to slip into the realm of numbness – of forgetting and denial. She felt herself to be dying and knew not why. What had she possibly done to deserve this? In her innocence and in her desperation, she let go and allowed the creeping numbness to take her over completely . . .

Δ   Δ   Δ   Δ   Δ   Δ

Later, much later, they came for her. The large spider people tied her up in sticky black ropes which bound her tight. They lulled her into even deeper sleep

30

with hypnotic songs sung in voices of melted velvet. Singing of entrancement and enchantment, of the bliss of oblivion. Then crude machines were brought forth and fastened to her temples and heart. Magnetic currents pushed back further her soul while obliterating all her memories.

The restructuring process continued. Inside her they spliced and reconnected, altering her celestial grid patterning to one of discord and distortion. Through it all, Kurala lay unaware, sleeping, dipping ever deeper into oblivion's abyss. It would be a long time before she had more tears to shed. Instead she was reprogrammed to learn hatred and deceit. A lust for power and control began to grow inside her. The manipulation continued until these insidious creatures succeeded, until finally Kurala became one of their own.

No, she did not resemble them in form. She was still a most beautiful woman, though a meanness and cruelty did she radiate, when at last, she awoke. Her dark hair was long and wavy; her mouth set and cold. Her eyes still did glitter, no longer with love, but with a raging sense of power. Yes, power was the key to everything. This is what she had become – power uncontrolled, untempered by wisdom or by love. Unbridled raw power desiring only to express itself by controlling others and amassing ever more power.

Kurala did not awaken gently, but was jabbed sharply with a prod. With this, she sat up suddenly, snarling, hissing, attacking. The spider people jumped back in admiration of the work they had done. Their new Queen had been prepared. Soon, they would present her to their King, the mighty Shamo. Maybe now he would no longer torture them by pulling off their legs and stunning them with prods.

You see, the spider people had been commanded by their King to capture and create for him a Queen. He

31

could not marry one of his own, for was it not true, that the spider women had a terrible reputation for killing their mates in the heat of passion and eating them? Hence Shamo had been determined to find a wife from some other realm to serve his needs. Even an Angel would do, in fact, that might give him greater prestige among his people! But, of course, Angels were too pure to live in this darkened sphere. So the trap had been placed in position until a victim was found. Then she had to undergo severe restructurization. But little did they realize, just what they had created . . . .

And high above
in the celestial heavens
an angel looked down,
carefully observing her sister,
and sadly wept
by the light of the stars . . .

Chapter Two:
SHAMO

Shamo sat alone in his Great Hall, dark eyes blazing in anticipation. His eight long, spindly, black fuzzy legs twitched nervously. There he sat, focusing his magnetic will, and waited . . .

Yes, Shamo was the ruler of Galaxitron. He had succeeded in making this small planet feared and hated throughout this vector of the galaxy. It had been all his doing, beginning back long ago when that wayward asteroid had collided with the planet. It was during that terrible moment of immense impact when the fissure had opened up. This jagged crack led downwards, deepwards, into a section of the dark netherworld which had been sealed shut for countless aeons. After the gigantic, unexpected collision, a fissure had traveled all the way down into a sealed pocket far underground.

After some arduous work of clearing away the debris, Shamo and his spider people had managed to escape the perpetual confinement of their sealed off world. Laboriously, they traversed the fissure until nearing the surface, they had to pause. Brilliant sunlight flooded their path, almost blinding them. Here, they were forced to wait for an extremely long time until their dark eyes finally adjusted to the sun's brightness.

Then the spider people emerged unto the planet's surface.

Until then Galaxitron had been a gentle and quiet place, not particularly noteworthy as planets go. It was peopled by small, peaceful, ethereal folk, somewhat akin to what you now call fairies. The bodies of these beings were composed solely of diffused webbings of Light. Not only were they transparent, almost disappearing into their surroundings, but their forms were perceivable only as an iridescent sheen.

Since they were such subtle, shimmering beings, used to living quietly alone on their tranquil planet, they had no use for protection or defensive measures, for indeed, they had never, ever, thought that a day might come in which danger would threaten them.

We shall call these beings the Whispers, which is the very best we can do. For their true name was such a subtle, whispery, merest hint of sound, that if I tried to put it into words, it just wouldn't do. Letters are simply too heavy and crude to express their name. They would crush it into the page, burying it under the mountainous weight of unnecessary sound. So the name, Whispers, shall do just fine for now.

Well, you can probably imagine what happened next, so I shall make it as brief as possible and spare you some of the grief . . .

One day – one ominous and terrible afternoon to be specific, Shamo and his spider people finally emerged onto the surface of Galaxitron. They stared with amazement at the shimmering delicateness before them. There was a music too, a subtle, sweet harmonic of bells and wind, shifting and glimmering – always changing, ever moving. A most rare and exquisitely beautiful world at play, innocently awaited them.

For several moments they stood transfixed, for never before had they beheld such a sight. They couldn't quite comprehend the sweet interplay of sound and shifting rainbow lights. Then as an involuntary shudder coursed through Shamo's being, he plunged into action. With a roaring growl, Shamo and his spider people rushed forth on their hairy black legs, waving sharp prods menacingly. Crushing and cutting to pieces as many of the unwitting Whispers as they could. It was a terrible sight, one that I would wish never repeated again. But, of course, such things have been experienced repeatedly throughout the numerous galaxies of this dimensional universe for it has long served as the playing field of duality.

Unspeakable indeed, was the horrible carnage on Galaxitron that fated day until finally, the music itself fell deathly silent. The Whispers had disappeared, except perhaps, for an iridescent patch on that leaf over there, or inside the center of a flower. Or if you looked carefully enough, you might discover a slight rainbow sheen on one of the stones hidden on the bottom of the river. But basically, the Whispers and their world had been destroyed.

When the crushing silence descended, the big, black spiders began to cheer, wildly dancing with total abandon. Soon, things got so crazy that they began to fight with each other, cutting and hacking and stinging. It took most of the night for things to settle down.

Thus it was that the Spider People of Shamo conquered the gentle Whispers of Galaxitron. You can find the complete history of this recorded within the Starry Chronicles kept within the Great Libraries on the planet Galador of the star system Mensa.

Many years later, the Shamo, as we shall call all of Shamo's people, had built their huge, slimy plum and lime green palace along with numerous catacombs linking the entire planet. This was when they began to turn their attention to invading other planets. Shortly after that, they experienced their first encounter with the Dark Lords of Orion.

ALL THE INFORMATION

BEING GIVEN TO YOU

IS LIKE A HOLOGRAM

IN WHICH YOU ARE SHOWN

ONLY ONE SMALL PIECE.

FROM THE SMALL PORTION

WHICH YOU HOLD,

YOU SHALL DISCOVER THAT

THIS IS YOUR KEY

TO UNDERSTANDING

THE MULTI-DIMENSIONAL REALITIES

OF THE WHOLENESS

INHERENT IN EACH FRAGMENT.

Chapter Three:
THE OMNI

Three foreboding figures stood silently before the throne of Shamo. They were dressed in all pervading black which seemed to magnetically draw into them the energy of their surroundings. They were a black hole unto themselves, altering the vibratory currents so they could suck everything into their own centers – which gave them ever more power. In their combined presence they formed a unit in which there was no sense of heart or humanity. They were immovable and unrelenting. Although from their physical appearance alone, they were not frightening, they exuded a most threatening presence, giving rise to feelings of deep terror in almost everyone whom they encountered. It was the dreaded triad known as the OMNI, the rulers of the Dark Lords of Orion.

The OMNI stood as one vast, impenetrable presence, although their three forms were quite different in physical appearance. The first of the three was short and overweight. His hair was cropped close to his head, making his squinty pale blue eyes stand out from the folds of flesh. They glinted with malice. This one was without a doubt the most impatient of the three. Even now he was fidgeting nervously, ready to lose his temper at the slightest provocation. On the far side, the third OMNI was tall and gaunt with straight hair pulled back. He had a finely chiseled bone structure and deep set hollow eyes which made his face resemble a skull. Quiet and imperious, he emanated coldness, cruelty and subtle manipulation. The OMNI in the center was the most intriguing, for he was extremely handsome and mysterious. His magnetic eyes radiated deep knowledge and although he was assuming a passive role in this visit, it was acknowledged by many that he held the supreme leadership over the three.

As they coldly stared at Shamo, even he the fearful King of the Spider People, felt himself drenched with the icy cold currents of fear. Shamo had to constantly realign himself in order to maintain any semblance of balance and control. As he carefully arranged and rearranged each of his skinny, black legs upon his throne, Shamo gazed at the OMNI with a faked, friendly, manipulative detachment. It took every effort of his will to keep his life force from rushing into their darkened vortex. He vainly wished that he only had to deal with one of them at a time, not with all three!

The first of the three began to speak in a low voice, whose penetrating rumble traveled throughout the palace, causing a shaking vibration, much like an earthquake.

"I am Triax of the OMNI. It has been observed that you have conquered the planet Galaxitron without our permission. This is most foolhardy, for we are the Lords and Overseers of much of Orion. Galaxitron lies within the sphere of influence of our recently acquired subsidiary of Draco, hence you must now answer to us, for we are all powerful. Bow down before us as your Lords and Masters or you shall be crushed without mercy. We can destroy you and your insignificant planet in an instant, so do not consider crossing us."

Throughout this discourse, Shamo listened impassively, his eyes like bottomless pools, carefully weighing his options to see whether he had any.

Triax continued, "If you are smart enough to submit to our omnipotent power and authority, we will grant you permission to remain on this planet. Of course, you shall be under our jurisdiction. We have some projects for you to do within this sector of your galaxy. Your cunning and cruelty will be put to good use. But don't ever try to delude yourself that you will be able to outwit us for we are far beyond your feeble powers of manipulation. Never forget that!"

To further punctuate his meaning, Triax pointed his chubby finger at Shamo, inducing an immediate, immense pain throughout Shamo's hairy body. As the spider King writhed around on his throne, a tightly controlled smile appeared on Triax's face. Then as suddenly as it had begun, the pain stopped.

Trembling with fear and hatred, Shamo lay back weakly upon his cushioned throne.

"I pledge myself and my people as loyal servants of the OMNI. We await your command," he stammered with a shaky voice.

"Most wise of you," Triax replied, "although we would enjoy pulling off your legs one by one if you need any more convincing."

Shamo's entire body began to shake so strongly that he emitted a rattling sound.

"Now that you have agreed to be part of our alliance, that won't be necessary. However, if you or any of your people ever dare to cross us, you can be sure of a horrendous punishment, worse than death itself!" Triax appeared to be genuinely enjoying himself. "What we want you to do is to subjugate some more planets. We will supply you with warships and weapons. This entire portion of the galaxy has not been explored by us. You are to conquer each planet and bring them into our control. You need not concern yourself with showing any degree of mercy to the inhabitants of these planets, just like you did here. However, you may take prisoners, if there are any who suit your purposes. We expect full and prompt reports on all of your activities. We have spies everywhere, so we will hear of everything anyway. Never dare to attempt to double-cross us!"

Again Triax pointed his finger at Shamo who felt the stabbing pain return. It was as if all his legs were being crushed at once.

When the pain had finally subsided, Shamo looked up from his place on the floor and saw that the OMNI had departed. And even Shamo, as fearless and cruel as he was, wondered at what he had agreed to – even he had never imagined that such a powerfully evil force had existed.

And thus it was that the Shamo entered into full alliance with the Dark Lords of Orion.

Chapter Four:
THE MEETING

Shamo's encounter with the OMNI had taken place long before Kurala's restructurization process was complete. While waiting impatiently for his bride to be prepared for him, he set to work training his spider people into a state of combat readiness. Their fearsome prods were augmented by laser darts and magnetic ray machines supplied by the lieutenants of the Dark Lords of Orion. Black, metallic space ships arrived which were fully stocked with the implements of war and the necessary provisions for extended space journeys.

The spider people were taught how to maneuver these ships through the twists and turns of the churning star currents. The Shamo were filled with great excitement while anticipating their future adventures and impending battles to conquer the galaxy. In fact there was such an abundance of activity, that Galaxitron became rather peaceful for a brief time. The normal course of violent arguments actually abated since there was so much to accomplish. *(But have not wars always served the purpose of diverting attention away from inner problems in order to meet an outer need?)*

Warships finally began to depart in all directions. The spider people clamored noisily to be chosen for battle. Fights sometimes broke out among the space travelers and those who had to remain behind. The Spider People had a fierce propensity for jealousy and competiveness. Shamo himself stayed on Galaxitron, although he too longed to experience the thrill of battle. He had much to do organizing the departing raiders and keeping the ones remaining behind from getting into too much trouble. Also, he knew that soon Kurala would be ready to meet him.

Shamo had been alone for a very long while. He wanted a woman badly, not so much for his physical needs, for he had learned to channel much of that energy into his work, but as someone he could work with intimately and share his plans with. Except for old Shakarr, he had never trusted any of his spider people for all of them were exceedingly jealous and cunning, although not to the degree that he was, which is what kept him in power. It was actually quite exhausting for him to keep himself so feared and hated by his people. It took a lot of energy and constant manipulation to remain in power. What Shamo wanted most of all was a confidant.

Thus it was that in the midst of the flurry of activity with warships departing almost daily, spiders being trained in martial arts, and the constant, all consuming task of keeping some semblance of order among the fractious spider people, that a message was sent to Shamo announcing Kurala's impending arrival.

After the messenger had departed, Shamo retired to his private quarters, dismissed his servants and closed the door tightly. There he began rapidly doing pushups as spiders are wont to do in times of tremendous excitement. Steadily, with fixed compulsion, Shamo's hairy body heaved up and down rhythmically, doing pushup after pushup. This continued until he had completed over 10,000 pushups, something of a record for any of the spider people, and a clear indication of the high degree of his excitement.

Shamo felt much calmer now and opening his door, bellowed for his servants to return. Eight young spider youths scurried inside and began brushing his furry legs with great care. They didn't dare pull one hair as that would bring an instant reprisal to them. Shamo wanted to look his very best to meet his future Queen this evening. He was sprayed heavily with the perfume of rotting orchids which was his special favorite and was used in great profusion throughout his palace.

After dining alone in his room on a luscious dish of exotic intergalactic insects, Shamo made his way to the throne room throbbing with anticipation. Carefully arranging himself upon his throne, Shamo took great care that none of his legs were sticking out at weird angles. He didn't want to frighten his bride, for she might not be initially attracted to spiders.

And then, something strange happened. For an instant, Shamo felt a shiver of deep fear penetrate his being. It was so powerful that he began to quiver involuntarily. It was a quiet quiver, unnoticable to the others, but the mighty Spider King was unable to control it.

That was the moment when Kurala entered the throne room. She stood surveying the entire scene from the far side of the room. He was struck instantly by her great beauty and then further attracted by her aura of haughty arrogance. As their eyes met, there was the glitter of mutual recognition. Truly, it could not be said that this was the first time they had met. And although it was impossible that they had met before, she having previously been an Angel in the Celestial Realms, and he having been sealed up under the planet – in that instant of recognition, both of them knew it to be true.

Kurala stared at Shamo with defiance and began to laugh. She had never seen anyone as funny as this extremely serious hairy black spider creature with a misshapen crown upon his head. Shamo had not been prepared for this. He had never before been laughed at or ridiculed. He had always been hated, feared and respected. For a minute he felt a rush of hatred for this beautiful woman, becoming so angry that he considered having her murdered on the spot. Standing up on his throne, he threw himself into doing some vigorous pushups to regain his composure.

This struck Kurala as even funnier and now she leaned weakly against the palace wall, shaking with laughter. Shamo's guards pressed upon her and motioned her forward to the throne, pushing her roughly down upon the floor with their ever present prods. Her laughter finally ceased as Shamo stopped doing his pushups and glared downwards at her.

"I am Shamo, the King of the Spider People!" he announced angrily. "I am your Lord and Master. You are pledged to eternal allegiance with me. And never again shall you laugh at me!" he screamed.

Rising slowly from her place on the floor, Kurala stood firmly in front of him. She spoke with a cold, withering authority. "I am Kurala and never shall anyone be my Lord and Master. You will yet discover which of us is the most powerful. But I may well be merciful towards you, since you are simply the funniest creature I have ever encountered."

And thus it was that the meeting took place between Shamo and Kurala. Possibly, it had been foreordained after all, for she brought to him the seeds of his downfall already well mixed with hers.

Chapter Five:
THE WEDDING

S hamo and Kurala were duly married with much pomp and ceremony. The wedding was attended by all the Spider People of Galaxitron, save those who were off warring among the planets. Everyone noted how ravishingly beautiful Kurala was. She wore a long clingy black dress of finely spun mesh, slit up the sides to her waist. Her hair was piled high upon her head adorned with purple orchids in varying stages of decay. Shamo grew weak at the sight of her. She was so gorgeous!

Kurala stood triumphantly surveying the Spider People, a small smile playing at the corners of her mouth. *(She found them quite comical, especially since they took everything so seriously.)* Her eyes glittered with superior knowledge. She had long ago forgotten that she was a prisoner or how she had originally arrived at Galaxitron. All she knew was that these silly, ignorant, hairy Spider People were about to crown her their Queen. *(And wasn't that extremely fitting!)*

Of course, in order to become Queen, she had to marry Shamo, but she had come to terms with that the first time she had met him. Although Shamo was not particularly attractive, unless you happened to be a spider woman, that did not matter to Kurala. What was important to her was power and currently Shamo held the power on Galaxitron. Naturally, that would soon change after she became Queen. Although he seemed to be held in respectful terror by his people, he certainly didn't frighten her!

Besides, she had already discovered that he had a few traits which she actually liked. Shamo had a sensuous side to him that she had not expected. She had never before been stroked and embraced by eight legs at once. Being with him helped to soothe her often overwrought and high-strung temperament. And she knew well that this foolish Spider King was madly in love with her and would do whatever she wished. Shamo's eyes constantly followed her with a look of shameless adoration. He heaped compliments on her and gave her anything she desired, so awed was he by her presence and beauty. Kurala loved this feeling of control.

The marriage ceremony continued on and on. Now a stringy haired spider woman was singing a dirge-like song while plucking a stringed instrument which droned on endlessly. Kurala sat regally upon her throne as if frozen in a dream. Shamo gazed at her in wonder. Finally, came the moment she had been waiting for. Shamo picked up a silver crown and placed it upon his wife's head. Kurala was now proclaimed to be Queen of Galaxitron. She arose in her full power and loomed above her subjects, smiling majestically. In the depth of her eyes was an expression of blankness which no one noticed save maybe an iridescent sheen here or there. Shamo stood beside her and proudly showed off his Queen. Both King and Queen of Galaxitron reveled in the glow of adoration. The spider people yelled and cheered with wild abandon, tapping their hairy feet in syncopation, sounding like an army of drummers.

This was to be Shamo's greatest moment of glory, for now that the net was cast, destiny began to unravel. The clever King of the Spiders had trapped himself with his pride by overstepping the boundaries of what is allowed by Universal Law.

Chapter Six:
CONQUERING PLANETS

Let us skip ahead a few years in galactic time. Shamo is fully engaged in numerous battles to conquer and subjugate planets. Warships depart Galaxitron every day filled with spider warriors anxious for battle. Of course, many of these warships never return, for the carnage is great. In spite of the heavy casualties of war, the spider people still clamor loudly to be sent off to war. They seem to crave the excitement and brutality of it. And as they multiply rapidly, their ranks are continuously being renewed by new legions of young spiders impatient to prove themselves.

Shamo has his hands full with his people, keeping them from totally running amok in the frenzy of excitement. Occasionally warships return with the wounded, most of whom are beyond healing. They are thrown into a dark corner of the palace grounds where they are given food and water and left to quietly die. Of course, the spider people don't do anything very quietly, so if you happen to pass by that quadrant of the palace you might hear a very loud wailing and cursing from the abandoned wounded.

Sometimes, victorious warships arrive laden with the spoils of war. Great treasures, works of art and beauteous jewels which the spider people don't quite know what to do with, so they are lumped in heaps and mounds outside the palace. Only Kurala has any appreciation of these things and sometimes she retrieves a necklace or a beautiful statue and puts it inside the palace.

Then there are the newly arrived slaves, mainly women of beauty who are given to the warriors as concubines. The few men who are brought here are chained together and put to work at jobs which the spider people disdain to do. Their lot is not a happy one, for they are beaten and tortured for the slightest transgression, imagined or real.

Shamo often goes off to war now that Kurala can keep order when he is gone. The spider people are afraid of her, even more so than of him and are always on their best behavior when left alone with her. She tolerates no disrespect, laziness or cleverness from them. The punishment is always the same, immediate death. Outside the palace, Kurala keeps a phalanx of bodyguards with her, available to execute anyone in an instant.

When she encountered the first prisoners of war, Kurala was shocked to see others with forms like her. She had assumed that, except for her, the universe was inhabited only by spiders. Staring intently at the women slaves, she became incensed if she considered them more beautiful than herself and often condemned them to death on the spot. These poor women could not understand how a woman like themselves could live amongst these horrible spiders and be so cruel!

It was the male prisoners who fascinated Kurala the most. Although many of them appeared downtrodden or broken in spirit, occasionally there would be one who would stare back at her with courageous astonishment. These she did not kill, but rather quietly observed, promising to herself to soon try out one as a lover.

Which she did, the very next time that Shamo was away. What a novelty it was to be with someone with only two legs! Of course, when Shamo returned and found out about the affair from his many spies in the palace who were only too eager to tell him, the poor, hapless lover was horribly tortured and killed. Kurala was amused by all the fuss, knowing that Shamo did not have the courage to confront her directly.

After awhile, Kurala began to get bored with the life on Galaxitron and announced to Shamo that she wanted to go off to war. He could stay home for a change. Not daring to cross her, for Shamo truly worshipped his wife, he reluctantly agreed.

Thus did Kurala develop into a wild warrioress. Her exploits are well chronicled and are probably already known to you. Increasingly, Shamo was left behind on Galaxitron to run the daily duties of the planet, while it was Kurala who commanded the fleet of warships. Although highly successful at the subjugation of minor planets, Kurala soon tired of this limited sphere of activity. Conquering peaceful and backward planets did not keep her adrenalin flowing sufficiently. She longed to be engaged in a real challenge. So Kurala began exploring beyond the boundaries set for them by the Dark Lords of Orion. This is when the trouble began in earnest.

Chapter Seven:
BETELGEUSE

Far away, in the great star system of Betelgeuse, the Council of Light was in secret session...

Betelgeuse was located in the constellation known as Orion though quite distant from the star system of Rigel, home of the Dark Lords. Orion has held the key patterning for this dimensional universe since its creation. It is the pivotal anchor point for duality, hence you will find within this one constellation both the darkest and lightest of energies, forever acting out the roles of good and evil with concentrated focus. Orion chose to embody this template of duality for all of us so we could fully experience matter, separation and illusion.

Halfway between Betelgeuse and Rigel there is a zone of overlap where the energies of light and dark have merged and through sacred, alchemical union have become One. Located within this zone are the three stars in the belt of Orion which we shall term the EL-AN-RA. These three starry doorways are the control points which pin this dimensional universe into positional alignment on the template of duality.

The central star, Al Nilam or AN is the major doorway to myriad dimensional universes, hence has always been a key point within our sphere of experience. It contains a direct trajectory into the next Great Central Sun System. **It could be said about AN that there are many doors in, but only one doorway out.** This is where you will find the All-Seeing Eye.

The Council of the Elohim has always been responsible for the three stars in the belt of Orion. This sacred zone of overlap is under the leadership of the mighty Angel, Lord Metatron. It is also the home of the horse-shoe shaped Council of Orion which is continually in session with endless debates on the nature of right and wrong. The Dark Lords sit on the left of the Council in their black robes while the Light Lords sit on the right in their robes of white. There is a constant interplay between dry intellectual discourses and heated arguments. It matters not what is taking place since no one listens to the other side.

The zone of overlap is strongly protected by the Council of the Elohim. Other than for the sole purpose of attending the Council of Orion, no one is allowed here without permission of the Elohim. Even the dreaded OMNI did not dare to intrude, for it was vastly protected by a band of such intense Light that no one could enter into it without dissolving.

However, the sword of Orion which functioned as a runway of Light into the stars of the belt was not so protected. Although the Dark Lords could not enter upon the sword itself, they could cause disturbance to those attempting to approach the runway's entrance based at the tip of the sword. Light ships were often attacked and destroyed as they tried to slip past the ships of the OMNI to enter onto the sword. Hence it was considered a mark of great skill to be able to slip past the dark ships of Rigel. This entailed lightning fast maneuvers after arriving from an unexpected, random trajectory. Star Commanders who had successfully completed this passage were given numerous awards and status among those of the Intergalactic Fleets. They were designated Triple Commanders for having successfully entered the three stars of the belt and were greatly sought after for missions of supreme importance requiring advanced levels of skillful precision.

The Council of Light itself, resided within a vast complex of white domed temples on a small, milky white planet. This planet was ever veiled in a mist of clouds so nothing upon the surface could be clearly perceived by those passing by. There were so many stars and planets within the star system of Betelgeuse that the Council's planet was well hidden. Indeed, this was meant to be. Even for those invited to visit the Council, no directions were given, save to meet at a distant star where you would be escorted into a windowless chamber on one of the Council's light ships. When the journey was complete, you would disembark directly into the Council complex itself.

Right now, a light ship has landed within the Council of Light and prepares to disengage its passengers. A tall, ruggedly handsome man with clear, sparkling eyes rises from his seat and walks confidently towards the doorway. He has visited the Council many times and is familiar with its procedures. A Council member greets him warmly at the door and leads him into the Council chambers.

As they enter, a hush descends upon the gathering. Many faces look at him with respect, for this man is AAla-dar, legendary Triple Commander par excellence from the Star System of Aldebaron. AAla-dar takes his seat quietly and joins in the silence as an attunement is made.

Uriel-la rises and begins to speak in a voice like flowing water. "Welcome to the Council of Light, beloved AAla-dar. We have called you here to discuss with you a matter of great concern. We have been receiving numerous reports of disturbances from sub sector F13 of the Draco System. Are you aware of any sightings of unidentified warships within that area?" Uriel-la's eyes are filled with compassion and responsibility, her face timelessly serene.

As AAla-dar arose, a murmur of admiration filled the Council chamber. He emanated a graceful vitality. Here was a man not only exceedingly capable, but who possessed the energy, wisdom and impeccability to successfully achieve the most difficult of tasks.

"Yes, I am. Our Star Command has felt numerous imbalances upon the rhythms of the star waves while passing through that sector. On occasion we have picked up survivors of some devastation. It appears that numerous planets are being conquered."

AAla-dar paused here while he allowed the memories of what he had witnessed to pass through his heart and be released. Although he had seen much in his long years as an Intergalactic Warrior, he had kept his heart open. Perhaps that was a sign of his greatness, that rare combination of humility, nobility and compassion. AAla-dar was strong and tough, but his eyes emanated tenderness and humor. Possibly, that's why so many women throughout the galaxies found him irresistibly charming. Even Uriel-la was delighted with his presence, although she had long ago merged her dualities into almost total androgyny.

AAla-dar continued, "We haven't yet been able to ascertain who is responsible for this carnage, except that the survivors spoke of horrible, large black spiders. What does the Council know of this?"

Antar-Ra spoke next: "We have discovered that these energies originate from a small planet in the Draco System called Galaxitron. It has been invaded by a group of spider beings called the Shamo who were previously sealed off into an underground cavern on the planet. However, when Galaxitron was hit by a wayward asteroid, the Shamo escaped and began their cycle of destruction. We are led to believe that the Shamo are now working with the OMNI. If so, the task before us will be even more difficult than usual. As you well know, the OMNI are not allowed to overstep their preordained boundaries of exploitation. And we are not allowed to deal directly with them at all. All that the Council of Light can do is to hold the focus of Light for this dimensional universe. So if there is a matter of impropriety it must be settled by others. That is why we have called upon you and the Intergalactic Confederation."

AAla-dar stiffened and raised himself into a higher awareness. "And what do you wish us to do?" he asked.

Uriel-la gave him a penetrating look. "We want you to go to the Shamo and communicate to them their breach of Universal Law."

"And if they don't wish to cooperate?"

"Then you must ascertain if they are working with the Dark Lords. If they are or if they are not, they must be stopped by whatever means at your disposal," Uriel-la replied calmly. "You are empowered by us to activate as many of the Intergalactic Fleets as you need to complete this task."

"And what if we have to take on the OMNI themselves?" AAla-dar asked, hardly daring to look at such a dire scenario.

"That cannot be. For a direct battle with the Dark Lords would only bring grief and suffering to everyone. It is a war which is impossible to win, either by them or by us. If that appears to be the only possibility, we shall have to discover another solution," Uriel-la stated firmly.

Another hush descended upon the Council chambers. The full seriousness of the situation before them was being deeply felt.

"AAla-dar," Uriel-la's starry eyes pierced into him again, this time transmitting to him a renewed sense of confidence and authority. "We have great trust in you. We know that you are the one to bring this matter to a successful conclusion."

The Star Commander bowed deeply to the assembled Council. "I will give it my full commitment. I shall do whatever is necessary." AAla-dar rose to his full height and strode from the Council of Light.

And thus it was that the scene was set for the beginning of the end.

Chapter Eight:
DENEB

AAla-dar returned to Aldebaron and immediately summoned the leaders of the Intergalactic Confederation. Sharing with them his experiences in the Council of Light, he asked for their help which was readily given. The finest, fastest starships of the fleet were placed at his disposal. Communications channels were activated and readied for the first signs of trouble. It was decided that he should take his best squadron to the Star System of Vega which was located near Draco and wait for an opportunity to encounter the invaders.

Utilizing the open direct channels through space which are now referred to as *worm holes*, they arrived at Vega with great haste. Here they were shown warm hospitality and offered full access to all the facilities of the Vega Starfleet. Then the word came, enemy warships had been sighted moving towards the star sector of Deneb. AAla-dar and his squadron hurried to their ships and took off, knowing that if they made haste, they would beat the invaders to Deneb.

By the time AAla-dar arrived at Deneb, the High Command had already been forewarned. He shared with them his plan. "While we are activating the fortifications here and preparing for war, we shall keep our preparations hidden. On the outside, we shall make it look as if we are caught unawares. When the invaders arrive, we will welcome them with great hospitality. It is important that I be given an opportunity to talk with their leader. Maybe then, we can avert a direct confrontation with the OMNI."

The High Command readily agreed to this plan. In the meantime the Vega Fleet was secreting itself on nearby planets ready to help out if needed.

Within a few days, the warships of Galaxitron were sighted. Soon the skies were filled with black warships. These rained down upon Deneb a laser display more frightening to look at, than actually destructive. Then a sleek black warship bearing the symbol of a single purple orchid landed.

AAla-dar was there, standing ready when it arrived. He watched as the hatch opened and several large, hairy, black spider people disembarked. They were truly ugly, but also somewhat comical swaggering down the gangplank weighed down by numerous prods and laser guns. The spider warriors descended in two lines, then stopped and looked back to the ship anxiously, as if waiting for approval. Within moments, a woman stepped forth confidently from the black craft – a ravishingly beautiful woman, a wildly independent woman, yet one who did indeed, emanate cruelty and arrogance.

AAla-dar had not expected his adversary to be a woman, especially not one this beautiful. Of course, he had done battle with female warriors before; there were many of them. But none of them had the combined power, beauty, intelligence or cunning of this one.

As he sized her up, she approached, gazing at him with astonishment. Never before had the inhabitants of a planet come out to greet them; they had always run away in fear like scared mice. Who was this man and why was he standing there so calmly, staring at her intently? Even Kurala could not help noticing that he was extremely handsome, capable and confidant. Her curiosity was aroused as it had never been before.

AAla-dar raised his hand to her in the Intergalactic Salute signifying peace and Oneness. "Greetings and welcome to Deneb, Vector 5. I am Commander AAla-dar of the Intergalactic Confederation."

Kurala was so surprised by his power and his poise that for once she was caught off guard and raised her hand to him in a quick copy of his gesture. "I am Kurala, Queen of Galaxitron and Conquerer of the Universe."

"Pleased to meet you, Your Highness," AAla-dar replied with an amused smile. "May I invite you to join me for a private counsel?" His charm must have been formidable indeed, for Kurala readily agreed to his invitation.

For some reason she had instantly trusted AAla-dar, recognizing his integrity, though she also instinctively knew that they were enemies and the time would probably soon come in which one of them would have to kill the other. Leaving behind her spider people, she haughtily walked through the space station with him to his private suite of apartments. "At least I won't be spied upon by spiders for awhile," she thought with relief.

As they passed by, everyone stared with surprise at this most powerfully attractive couple. Surely AAla-dar had met his match and better be quite careful in his dealings with her.

Chapter Nine:
ALONE TOGETHER

K urala gave a quick, but perceptive glance around her. Never before had she seen such luxury! The apartment was beautiful. It was filled with azure light from an unseen source and there was a pool of water in the center of the floor. Dipping her fingers into it, she noted its perfect temperature. Best of all, there was no smell of rotting orchids which she had grown quite sick of! There was such a freshness to everything which was new to Kurala.

AAla-dar watched her astonishment at her surroundings although both of them carefully tried to mask their perceptions from the other. As this was simply a regulation guest apartment in a space station and not very fancy at all, he correctly surmised that wherever she came from must be a very poor and unenlightened planet. He gestured for her to sit on a soft lavender couch and brought her a goblet of sparkling amethyst wine.

"Kurala, would you care for something to eat? We have fruit from several star systems here and wafers from Vega, or possibly you would like something prepared for you from the skyport kitchen?"

Kurala was hungry, but she had never tasted fruit

or wafers and didn't know what they were. She had tried some of the food from the small planets they had conquered, but had not found it to her liking. "Do you have any insects?" she asked.

"Insects?" AAla-dar quickly covered up his surprise that this beautiful woman *ate insects!* "I don't know, but I'll ask the kitchen." He called the kitchen which was as unprepared as he was for this request. "I'm sorry, but they are all out of insects today," he apologized. Of course, spiders ate insects, he had forgotten.

"Do they have any flies?" she asked with a degree of impatience.

He called the kitchen again and they didn't have any flies. "No flies, but possibly you might try some of this fruit, it's really quite tasty." AAla-dar grabbed a piece of angel fruit off the tray and handed it to her.

Kurala recoiled from it, an involuntary tremor passing through her body. "No, I can't have that. I'll try one of the wafers from Vega." She took some tentative nibbles from the wafer and found it simply the most delicious thing she had ever eaten. Soon, she had eaten all of the Vega wafers and drunk two glasses of amethyst wine. Some of the hardness began to soften from her face. And AAla-dar found her even more beautiful and fascinating. He would have to be most careful to keep focused on his duty. He had to remember that she was a ruthless invader who might attack him at any time.

She certainly didn't appear to be ruthless right now. Kurala was showering him with questions about his experiences. "What was the Intergalactic Confederation?" "Where did he come from?" "What kind of ships did they have?" "Did he conquer planets too?" She was sorry that he didn't, because she had thought that if he did, maybe they could go off to war together. "How far had he traveled?" "What was a Triple Commander?"

"Was he married?" He was not, but he found out that she was, to the King of the Shamo. How could this woman marry a spider?

Then AAla-dar asked her a few questions. Kurala told him all about Galaxitron, but knew nothing about her origins before arriving there. She had no memories of anything before that, and had never thought about it before. He assured her that since she was not a spider, she must have come from somewhere else, possibly she had gotten lost or captured and her memories had been erased. This gave Kurala something new to think about and she resolved to ask Shamo about her true origins as soon as she returned to Galaxitron.

The wine flowed freely and they had already eaten two more deliveries of Vega wafers. They now felt like comfortable friends with visible sparks of energy passing freely between them. Their yearnings brought them closer together until AAla-dar took her in his arms and kissed her with the fullness of his unleashed passion. Kurala didn't hesitate as she felt a great hunger well up inside of her and gave herself to him as she had never done before. AAla-dar had never experienced anyone like this woman who was his equal on so many levels. He had waited a long time for someone like her.

Thus passed an evening of great love and tender passion, a new experience for both of them. In the morning AAla-dar awoke with Kurala still lying in his arms, tenderly wrapped around him as if he was her lifeline. Still drowsy with sleep they reached for the other, lips hungrily seeking out lips, kissing each other as if they would never kiss again, fully expressing the deep alignment within their hearts.

After bathing in the pool which Kurala loved, especially when they started playfully splashing each other, and dressing, they had more wafers delivered for breakfast. The kitchen proudly informed AAla-dar that it had now obtained some flies and insects for their guest. But Kurala wanted only Vega wafers for they reminded her of AAla-dar.

In between bites of wafers, Kurala was full of questions while AAla-dar laughed in delight. Then she asked him if he was in allegiance with the Dark Lords of Orion like they were. AAla-dar stopped in mid-laugh as a wave of sadness rolled into his heart like a heavy fog.

"No, I am not. Are you really in alliance with the OMNI?" he asked, hoping that he had misunderstood her question.

"Of course, we are. How could we not be? They are all-powerful," she replied.

"Kurala, there are many forces at play in this dimensional universe and the OMNI are just one of them," AAla-dar explained quietly.

"But who is a more powerful force of evil than the OMNI?" she asked with much surprise.

"The OMNI are the most powerful of the dark forces, but there are also forces of Light, with which I am aligned."

"Well, if the OMNI are the strongest of the dark forces, then it's perfect that we're aligned with them," Kurala stated with obvious relief.

"No, Kurala, it's not. Why do you want to align yourself with dark energies anyway? You are so beautiful, so talented, you should use your energies in service to the Light," he replied with force.

"Service to the Light? You must be joking!" Kurala began to laugh and a meanness began to return to her countenance.

"I don't understand what you find funny about serving the Light!" AAla-dar retorted.

"Look, I'm not here to be in service. I'm here to conquer and control, to amass power until I become more powerful than the Dark Lords of Orion! I plan to have the entire universe in *my* control someday," she replied.

"Kurala, you're crazy. No one can conquer the OMNI, no one. Even the combined Intergalactic Confederation can't do it. It's because the OMNI chose to take on the task of embodying the dark force in this dimensional universe of duality. Hence they're invincible. You'd be out of your mind to even consider taking them on. If you align yourself to the dark energies, you'll always be under their control." AAla-dar wanted desperately for her to understand and to shift her energies away from such a doomed path.

"No one will ever control me. Never! They might think that they have me under their control, but they never will," Kurala said with vehemence.

"Look Kurala, the OMNI are a lot more heavy and ruthless than you and your spider people. You have no idea what you're getting yourself into. I wish you'd listen to me. I have a lot of experience in these matters."

"AAla-dar, stop trying to tell me what to do. I'm fully capable of making my own decisions. I'm certainly not going to stop invading planets just because *you* don't like it!" Kurala was getting angry now. She pushed him away from her.

AAla-dar was not happy with the direction of their conversation. It was getting progressively worse. What had happened to the closeness between them? Here he was with the woman of his dreams and she was fast turning into a nightmare. And he wasn't doing what he had come here to do, which was to convince her to stop transgressing on other planets. And if she didn't, then he personally would have to stop her.

He sat quietly lost in his thoughts. Then time appeared to stop as a moment of deep peace and stillness descended upon them. "Ah," thought AAla-dar, "an Angel must be passing by overhead." He had temporarily forgotten that he was not alone with Kurala. Was he not always aided by the Council of Light! They had probably been monitoring him all along and had seen everything, including AAla-dar the famous lover, as well as the AAla-dar who was not doing his job of vanquishing these invaders very well. Uriel-la's face appeared before him for an instant. She gave him a piercingly stern look out of very twinkling eyes, smiled, winked and was gone. At least, she still had confidence in him! The moment of silence continued. "This must be an entire Legion of Angels!" AAla-dar observed.

"Kurala..." "AAla-dar..." They both spoke simultaneously, turning towards each other as if drawn together by some secret chemistry. Each one's eyes mirrored the pain and sadness of the other. There was strong love between them; they both knew that, but would not, could not acknowledge it.

"Kurala, you must leave this planet now. I will allow you and your spider people safe passage back to Galaxitron. We have massive forces deployed here who can destroy your entire landing party in just a few moments." AAla-dar could not believe what he was doing, but he simply had to. Remember, he had integrity and honor. "The next time that we encounter any of your warships, we shall blast them out of the skies. I am commissioned under orders from the Intergalactic Confederation to inform you that you are transgressing Universal Law."

The woman stared at him with mute comprehension; she seemed to be undergoing an intense inner turmoil. Kurala started to speak, but could not.

AAla-dar brought her into his arms and kissed her a final time with forceful tenderness. She melted into him for a moment, then pulled herself away. Her eyes were filled with tears for the very first time.

"If you should ever decide to align yourself with the Forces of Light, look me up! I'll protect you even against the dreaded OMNI," he avowed with a churning heart. "Come, I'll see you to your ship now."

And thus it was that Kurala and AAla-dar did encounter one another and discover their fated, tragic love.

And high above
in the celestial heavens
an Angel looked down
upon her sister,
and sadly wept
by the light of the stars . . .

Chapter Ten:
THE RETURN

Re-entering her warship, Kurala made great haste to depart, shouting rapid orders at all the spider people. Her entire body was trembling; inside she had been shaken to the core. She must get out of here fast!

After what seemed to be a series of endless delays, they were finally airborne, rising almost vertically into the sky with a screaming sound, pushing their warships to top speed as if they were being pursued by enemy forces. But Kurala knew that they would not be attacked. Undoubtedly they were being subtly followed to ensure that they were truly returning to Galaxitron. After they were safely out of Deneb's forcefield, she had the fleet slow down to a normal pace for there was no reason to burn out the engines. Then she retired to her quarters leaving strict orders that she was not to be disturbed.

Here she stared for a long time into a small golden mirror which was one of the spoils of war she had captured. Did she look different? She certainly felt not the same as before. What was happening to her? Was she becoming weak? Had AAla-dar placed some sort of magical spell upon her? Kurala quickly dismissed that possibility, for she knew that in spite of everything,

AAla-dar was an honorable man. She had never met anyone with honor before – had never felt it to be an important quality. She certainly did not consider herself to be honorable and it wouldn't serve her to be so. "Just try being honorable on Galaxitron, you wouldn't last long," she thought bitterly.

Kurala knew that she was in love with AAla-dar. It hit her with an overwhelming certainty as she gazed into her own eyes. But she was also aware that if she met him again, he would try to stop her unless she stopped him first. Of course, she could always change her ways, but some terrible, secret thing inside gnawed at her, scraped against her heart, pressed against her brain with a relentless pain. This pain was only alleviated somewhat when she was being cruel and ruthless. She couldn't stand living with it; it needed to be fed constantly. No, she couldn't change her ways, that horrible beast inside would destroy her.

Kurala was getting hungry. She craved some Vega wafers and even briefly considered the possibly of invading some small unsuspecting planet in search of some wafers. But no, AAla-dar would be watching her and besides, she had better get used to insects again, that's all they have to eat on Galaxitron.

She was becoming increasingly anxious to return home. One of the first things she was going to do was to demand that Shamo reveal her true origin. "AAla-dar has changed me greatly, whether I like it or not," she thought angrily.

At last, she curled up on her sleeping mat and fell asleep dreaming about Triple Commanders and stargates, Vega wafers and tender kisses.

Chapter Eleven:
GALAXITRON

When she awoke they were almost home. Kurala jumped up and pulled herself together. She redid her hair so it would look more severe, pulling it back tightly and clothed herself in her heavy purple armor. Returning to the command deck, she glanced out the windows at Galaxitron and noticed that scattered areas of the planet appeared to be blackened and smoking. "What was Shamo up to now?" she thought to herself.

Upon arrival, she was greeted by Shakarr, the only one of the spider people whom Shamo trusted. Old Shakarr had been crippled in one of the early battles, but had somehow returned to health in spite of the fact that he now had only five usable legs. Shakarr served as Shamo's main assistant. He quietly urged her to make haste and follow him. They drove off in one of the small command modules which took them rapidly to the hideous lime green and plum palace. "Here's home," she thought to herself bitterly, thinking longingly of that exquisite apartment on Deneb.

The palace was unnaturally quiet. The pervasive smell of rotting orchids overwhelmed her; she almost became nauseated by the stench. Kurala paused for a moment to settle her stomach, but was pushed forward towards Shamo's private quarters by the insistent Shakarr. Ten guards stood on duty outside Shamo's room, rather unusual since he usually only had one. They stepped aside and let Kurala pass through the door which closed softly behind her.

Inside all was in darkness, deep darkness, in which she could see nothing. There was a heavy silence except for the sound of labored breathing. Kurala moved quietly to a window and folded back a corner of the curtain to allow a little light in, so she could see. She had never fully adjusted her eyes to complete darkness like the spider people. This was one of her weaknesses with them, although they had yet to discover it.

She saw Shamo lying upon his bed and quickly rushed to his side. His dark eyes glared out at her painfully. For an instant she thought that he had found out about her night with AAla-dar and gone into a black rage, but no, Shamo himself, was in deep pain. Something terrible had happened to him! Embedded into his forehead was a black metal box. From this box protruded metal coils which were stuck into his temples and the back of his head. More wires ran down his back and chest, attached at certain points with what appeared to be small transistors. Kurala was horrified to see that these wires disappeared right into his body!

"Shamo, what has happened to you?" she cried.

"Im-plants," he replied hoarsely.

"Who did this to you?" Kurala asked with a rising sense of terror.

"The OM-NI. They al-so bombed scat-tered areas of our plan-et."

"Oh, no! Why did they do this to you?" Kurala was becoming enraged. How dare they mutilate her husband in this way!

"Be-cause we dis-obeyed them by in-vading planets out-side of the pre-scribed bound-aries they set for us,"

Shamo said weakly. He was obviously in tremendous pain and had much difficulty breathing. "Act-ually, you are the one who was go-ing out-side the lim-its, I nev-er did. But I cov-ered up for you."

Kurala felt a flutter of compassion inside her for this poor, wretched spider king. She gently stroked one of his hairy legs. "Oh, Shamo, I'm so sorry that you've had to suffer so." What was happening to her; why was she softening up? How would she ever be a decent warrior this way? "Shamo, don't we have someone here who can heal you?"

"We don't have heal-ers on Gal-axi-tron. My people don't know how to heal; they on-ly know how to des-troy," Shamo replied with much effort.

"Well, don't they have healers on some of the planets we have conquered?" she asked.

"Yes, of course, but we al-ways kill them right a-way so they can't care for their wound-ed." Shamo was getting tired from all this talking. He looked so frail and pained. And Kurala realized that she needed time alone to think. Too much was happening too fast. So she made him as comfortable as she could, bid him rest and retired to her quarters as quickly as possible.

Entering her rooms, she noticed how dingy they appeared. As soon as she had some free time, she would go through the mounds of treasures heaped outside to see what could brighten up her surroundings. Next she turned her attention to contemplation, for she had learned much this morning.

First, Kurala resolved that the next time she invaded a planet she would order that all healers be taken prisoner. "We could use several healers on Galaxitron, maybe they could cure our wounded so they wouldn't make such a wretched racket while they are dying. And it would probably be a good idea to have a healer on my warship as well," she mused. But then there was the problem of trust, what if the healers sabotaged the injured instead of curing them? Well, she would simply find healers with honor. AAla-dar had honor and although he was her enemy, he had proven trustworthy. At least on their first encounter, who knows about their next... Yet, Kurala knew that AAla-dar would always be honorable with her, even if he killed her, he would do it with integrity, not by subterfuge or deceit. Of course, she could not promise the same for herself, could she?

Kurala forced herself to stop thinking about AAla-dar. There was too much to do. What was she going to do about the OMNI? The Shamo definitely weren't strong enough to attack them directly. What she needed to do was to create an invincible fighting force. This meant that she would have to send out secret summons throughout the galaxy finding the renegades and outlaws who would be willing to join with her. Maybe she could liberate some of the small planets they had invaded if they were willing to join the fight against the OMNI. Too bad that AAla-dar wouldn't join his forces with hers, surely overthrowing the Dark Lords would be serving the good. Maybe when he saw her strength and power, he would bring the Intergalactic Confederation to help. But, she knew that she couldn't count on him. Besides, there was always the possibility that he would try to stop her.

Kurala's mind was made up. She vowed to destroy the OMNI, whatever it took. Even if she now had two formidable opponents, both AAla-dar and the Dark Lords, she was not frightened. Rushing from her quarters, she made haste to prepare for the horrible times to come.

And thus the stage was set for the intergalactic wars.

Chapter Twelve:
MALDON

Kurala set upon achieving her goal with focused resolve. Meeting with Shakarr, she alerted him to her plan. Dear Shakarr was so devoted to Shamo for showing him kindness and saving his life, that even though he was terrified to do anything against the OMNI, he agreed to help serve Kurala. He knew well that if the Dark Lords were not vanquished, that the Shamo would never be safe from their terrible threats and revenge.

Together, Kurala and Shakarr secretly met with a group of their captives from other planets and promised them freedom if they would join their cause. This was quickly accepted by them, for they knew that this was their only chance for liberation. Soon after, the freed captives were quietly given ships and supplies and sent forth on missions to all of the planets which Galaxitron had conquered to gather together a vast fighting force.

All of this was done under a cloak of utmost secrecy, for Kurala still distrusted most of the spider people. She knew that when the time came, that they would fight fiercely alongside them against the OMNI, but she didn't want to risk revealing their plans before the time was ripe. In the meantime, she still sent forth war parties of spider people to conquer small, insignificant planets, in order not to arouse anyone's suspicion.

Shamo was not told about any of this. Both Kurala and Shakarr agreed on this matter. He remained in extreme pain and spent most of his time moaning and writhing about in his bed. Kurala would visit Shamo several times a day, sitting solicitously at his bedside, stroking his furry black legs. She was appalled by the presence of his Orion implants. Every time that she looked at them, it renewed her will to fight the dreaded OMNI. Kurala murmured to him that soon he would be healed, for indeed, she had sent messengers forth to bring back to Galaxitron the finest healers who could be found.

During this period of preparation, Kurala was given little time to think about AAla-dar. Yet his memory would emerge into her consciousness at the most unexpected times. Sometimes, it appeared as if he resided within her. His handsome face would shine with love; she would see his starry eyes cajoling her to serve the Light.

Her response to this depended upon her mood as well as her outer activities at the moment. Sometimes she would flash an angry reply at him. "Go away, leave me alone! I have chosen the task that you and your Intergalactic Confederation should have taken on." At other, quieter moments, she would allow herself to bask in his love, calling for him to give her strength and support. On occasion, she would wonder if there was any way they could ever be together.

Right now, she had much to think about. Thus her attention turned to the immediate problem, which was that they needed a vast arsenal of weapons and ships. How were they to obtain these? She had heard of a wayward planet full of outcasts and outlaws called Maldon and made ready for a surreptitious visit there. If she could obtain their assistance, possibly they could help her.

Information about Maldon was not difficult to gather. Everyone seemed to have heard numerous stories of the wild exploits of the Maldon renegade squadrons. While both spider people and captives regaled her and Shakarr with tales of the Maldon exploits and ruthlessness, Kurala could find no one who had actually been there. The planet was located in a remote quadrant of Vector 5, not near anything of significance. And apparently, even the OMNI left it alone. This information further piqued Kurala's interest and she made haste to prepare for her journey.

Not knowing what to expect, she gathered together some of the brightest of their war spoils as possible gifts. She also took along some of their most advanced weaponry for her personal use, if necessary. With a full awareness that the success of this mission depended largely on the impression that she made, rather than brute force, she packed her most alluring garments for the trip.

With the absolute minimal crew of spider people and captives that she could get by on, Kurala departed for the renegade planet of Maldon. The journey itself passed by with relative ease until they finally entered the boundaries of Maldon's quadrant. Then, without warning, two motley looking ships appeared from out of nowhere. They were painted in wild camouflage colors, covered with starry graffiti, looking like they had been put together from spare parts in a junkyard. Yet, they were the fastest ships she had ever encountered!

The renegade ships zoomed by the Galaxitron craft from both sides, cutting across their ship at weird diagonal angles, forcing them to slow down to almost nothing. As the ships cut closer and closer to them, Kurala shouted to her crew to bring their ship to hover position.

"So they want to play it tough with us, do they,"

Kurala whispered with excitement. "This is not quite the welcome I expected."

She personally took over the ship's controls. Her features tensed with concentration as she waited for the right instant to act. Nearly forgetting to breathe, she sat with her hand ready upon the hyperspace throttle. Here they came again, even nearer. This time she could feel the oscillating air currents of the passing ships bombard her craft. Then she acted. With split second precision, she activated both hyperspace and reverse simultaneously. This, she had never done before and wasn't quite sure if it would work. But actually, Kurala had discovered an old secret used by the Triple Commanders for entering Orion's sword.

Without a second's hesitation, she slammed the ship into forward and then after the briefest of pauses, out of hyperspace. There just ahead of them loomed the planet Maldon. If she had traveled another instant in hyperspace, their ship would have rammed right into it. Instead, the craft from Galaxitron made a graceful, swooping arc over the spaceport, then delicately landed as if it had been a normal, unhurried entry.

None of these maneuvers escaped notice on Maldon. There had been nods of approval and scattered cheering in the Maldon control tower when the strange black ship with the purple orchid had escaped their scout ships. The outcasts of Maldon had great respect for anyone with guts and independence. Now they were curious and a small cluster of them stood waiting for the landing party to disembark.

Kurala took her time. First she ordered her crew to remain aboard ship no matter what happened, then she retired to her quarters and put on a long, seductively filmy, purple mesh dress. Pinning up her hair, she added some sparkling, purple crystal earrings she had found sifting through the treasure piles on Galaxitron.

She looked gorgeous and she knew it. The final addition to her outfit was an Orion laser stunner tied around her hips. Now Kurala was ready.

By this time the Maldon onlookers were becoming impatient. They were starting to get rowdy and were about to shoot some holes into the Galaxitron ship for their amusement. Just in time, the hatch opened and Kurala appeared. She walked toward them radiating confidence, power, and beauty. Well frankly, she just took their breath away. None of them had ever seen anyone like her! They were speechless in their surprise and admiration.

Kurala was totally enjoying the profound effect she was making. She made the most of it, walking with an exaggerated languid grace. Ahead of her was the most unusual group of beings she had ever encountered. She carefully scanned each one of them while she made her approach. The Maldons were dressed in a wild assortment of fluorescent colored jump suits. Many of them had well worn cowboy boots on; it seemed to be some sort of badge of honor. Several were wearing battered cowboy hats and wrap-around sunglasses. Most of them were in human forms, but there were a few who had beaks and feathers and others who were covered in shaggy, animal fur. She smoothly masked her astonishment as she walked on.

Flashing them her most dazzling smile, Kurala graciously held out her hand to be kissed. (Looking back on this scene later, she didn't know where she had learned this gesture. Certainly not on Galaxitron.) Several Maldonians, who were obviously hardened, ruthless ex-Star Commanders stepped forward and kissed her hand with respect.

"Well, Gentlemen, are we ready to talk?" Kurala said sweetly while indicating to them that she wished to be taken inside.

Chapter Thirteen: THE COWBOYS

Thirteen of the meanest, wildest Maldon outlaws sat in a circle around Kurala, savoring her beauty, relishing her ruthlessness. Kurala had won them over before she even had begun to speak. They broke the ice by offering her a drink. Kurala didn't know what to ask for, even though it was apparent that they probably had the best stocked bar in the galaxy. After lots of ribald discussion and much swigging of various drinks amongst themselves, the Maldon cowboys decided to serve her Pleiadian champagne, which was obviously a great delicacy, although she had never heard of it before.

After a few sips of this bubbling, iridescent liquid, Kurala asked if they possibly had any Vega wafers. *(She wasn't going to show how backward she was and ask for insects this time!)* These were readily procured for her. Taking a delicious bite of her first wafer, Kurala was flooded with tender memories of AAla-dar and had to forcibly focus her attention back to the matters at hand.

The leader of this group was a man named Quintron. He was a feisty, tough ex-Star Commander who had obviously seen a lot of action, good looking in a sort of weathered way. This man had definitely been around and didn't get duped easily. He also had little tolerance for fools. Quintron obviously had trouble following higher authorities and had been asked to leave the

Intergalactic Confederation. This didn't seem to bother him much, instead he assumed an air of arrogance and acted as if he was proud to be a renegade. But Kurala could tell that inside him was a soft heart. He had already melted like butter around her. But she definitely wouldn't like to be one of his enemies either as he would prove to be a formidable opponent.

After sharing many stories of their exploits with her, Quintron turned to Kurala and fixed her with a piercing stare.

"O.K. baby, why did you come here?" he asked in a low voice.

Kurala replied without flinching, matching him stare for stare, "Because I want to work with you. We are preparing to go to war against the Dark Lords of Orion. We need all the help we can get, and you guys are the best."

"Why do you think we would be stupid enough to take on the OMNI?" Quintron challenged.

"It's not a question of stupidity. Look, we both know that you are smart enough to fight them *and* be victorious! This isn't a matter of gaining more wealth; I can see that you have quite enough of that. You can get anything you want. But it is a matter of pride and honor." *(There was that word again. How come she kept running into people with honor, when she didn't have any?)* "Look, I can tell that the Intergalactic Confederation doesn't hold you in a lot of respect. Did you ever wonder why? Maybe it's simple jealousy. Maybe it's because you're all better warriors than they are, and a lot braver too."

This statement was greeted with dead silence, but Kurala felt that they were listening and had been touched in one of their sore spots. She continued on while carefully choosing her words. "Have you ever wondered why the mighty Intergalactic Confederation has never taken on the OMNI? Maybe they're afraid of them, scared that they would lose the war. But I'm not afraid, and I'm only a woman. Don't tell me that you big, strong men are frightened of them too?"

Quintron bristled with rage while several others had to be restrained from getting into a brawl. Perhaps she had gone too far. Kurala took another sip of her champagne and waited for things to settle down.

Gradually calming himself, Quintron was lost in deep thought for several moments. Finally he spoke. "O.K. lady, we've got to sleep on this one and talk it over. This isn't something you just make a snap decision about. Taking on the Dark Lords is pretty heavy stuff. I'll escort you back to your ship for the night and we'll get together again in the morning. You need any food or anything?"

She had been hoping that he would ask. "I would love a few packages of Vega wafers, if you could spare any."

"Sure, easy. Hey, Kowtron, could you get some wafers for this lady?"

Kowtron, whose shaggy body was covered with black and white patches like a cow, hurriedly filled this request. Then Kurala graciously thanked them for their warm hospitality, treating each of them like respected gentlemen, showering them with love sprinkled with doses of flirtation.

On the walk back to her ship, Quintron took Kurala by the arm. He was even more serious than Shamo had been, she thought to herself. Yet, she truly liked the commander. She could tell that he had a powerful will and capability that would come in handy should they decide to join with her.

Pausing before her ship, Quintron again fixed her with his gaze. "Do you really know what you're getting yourself into, baby?"

"Yes, of course I do or I wouldn't be doing it," she replied evenly.

"Well, I'll see you in the morning, sleep well." Quintron gave her a quick kiss on the mouth, tipped his cowboy hat and was gone.

With a bemused smile, Kurala entered her ship, going immediately to her private quarters. She tore open the first box of Vega wafers and began stuffing them into her mouth in rapid succession until she remembered that she had only a limited supply and had better ration them for now.

As she quieted herself down to review the day, Quintron's parting words kept coming back to her. *"Do you really know what you're getting yourself into, baby?"* And now it hit her like a gigantic shock. Maybe she didn't know what she was getting herself into! She remembered how naive she had been when she met AAla-dar. How little experience she had really had in the real world. Why she still didn't know her true origins and hadn't been able to ask Shamo because he was always in so much pain. What if the OMNI put implants like that into her?

Kurala was becoming increasingly distressed and confused. Doubts and fear engulfed her like sprouting weeds, until finally, thoroughly worn out, she fell into a troubled sleep.

Chapter Fourteen:
THE DECISION

Early in the morning Kurala awoke, still full of concern. She searched for a way out of the morass she had created. What was this rising sense of dread? She had never experienced fear before. Was this a trick of the OMNI or was she finally coming to her senses? Carefully considering her options, she realized that if she didn't battle the OMNI that they would destroy Galaxitron. She was no longer willing to serve as their indentured vassal. AAla-dar had offered to protect her against the Dark Lords, but would he really be able to? And where did the Intergalactic Confederation fit in? What side would they choose to align themselves with? If she knew for sure that they would help her, she wouldn't feel so overwhelmed.

Finally, she reached some sort of resolution. She would abide by whatever Maldon decided to do. If they were willing to aid her, she would go ahead with her plans; if not, she would try to send a message to AAla-dar asking for his help and protection. If Quintron arrived this morning with offers of aid and she told them that she had changed her mind and was returning home like a scared rabbit, she would never hear the end of it. All her credibility would be lost. That's if they didn't become violent with her. She knew that they could always turn her in to the OMNI as a traitor for a handsome reward or a needed favor.

While sorting through her thoughts, Kurala was dressing in a fetching dress of flaming red, knowing that it would drive Quintron wild with desire. She had considered taking him on as a lover for she knew that he was greatly attracted to her, but decided to remain tantalizingly out of reach. It would serve her purpose better if they decided to be allies. It's always good to have a little sexual tension and excitement to liven things up, keep them wanting more of me.

Soon Quintron did arrive, and when he saw her his heart leapt. He lost his composure for a moment while he stared at her with lusty appreciation.

"Oh baby, you're really something," he drawled while pulling her into his arms and kissing her forcefully.

Kurala briefly returned his passion, then slowly drew away, not quite removing herself from his arms. "Good morning, Quintron. My, you're looking good today. Shall we go somewhere and get down to business."

Once again offering her his arm, Quintron led Kurala to the same room where they had met yesterday. The others had already assembled and were well established with drinking various brews. They offered Kurala some Pleiadian champagne and Vega wafers which she munched on with delight while thinking to herself that these outlaws were fun to be with. Then she waited to hear their decision.

Quintron began in his low drawl, "Well, we stayed up most of the night considering your offer. Look lady, we want to get one thing straight right off. We don't have to prove ourselves to anybody – not to you, not to the stinking Confederation, not even to the OMNI. You got that?"

Kurala nodded her head in approval. She was listening quietly, feeling strangely detached from whatever the outcome would be.

"Now that we got that little matter straightened out, we can get on to business," Quintron continued. "We have decided to help you in your war against the Dark Lords simply because, frankly, we've been a little bored lately and we love a challenge. And this is a big, juicy challenge, if ever there was one! Hell, maybe we're all crazy, you included, but at least we'll all die taking on a big one." Quintron laughed ruefully, "Now what do you need?"

Masking her surprise that they were actually going to help her, Kurala answered calmly, "We need a vast fleet of warships and arsenals of weapons for starters. I've been gathering an army from the planets we've conquered, but we still need more warriors, especially some with experience."

"O.K. We know where there is a supply depot of the Confederation that is lightly guarded. That will be easy to knock off. We can do that ourselves, but we'll need some extra pilots for the ships we capture," Quintron said.

"I'll send them to you as soon as I return," Kurala promised. "But you better let them into your quadrant without harassing them like you did me." She stared at him with authority.

"Look, lady, if we give our word, you can trust us. Haven't you ever heard about the honor among thieves?" At this remark, all the outlaws began laughing uproariously.

"I trust you completely, Quintron," Kurala replied with a nervous smile.

"Good. We're going to send Kowtron and Textron with you so they can help to train your forces. Now it's important that we keep our preparations secret, the

OMNI have spies everywhere, except here of course."
Again loud laughter ensued amongst the outlaws.
Quintron continued, "And the Confederation ain't going to be too happy when their supply depot is sacked,
so we better look out for reprisals from them as well. I'll
be in touch with you as soon as we're ready to make oui
first moves against the Dark Lords."

Kurala thanked them for their help, and clutching
her package of Vega wafers, prepared to depart with
Kowtron and Textron. She glanced over at Quintron to
say good-bye, but he was busy talking to some of the
other outlaws and didn't notice her.

"Quintron!"

He glanced her way. "Yeah?"

"Goodbye. I'll see you later," she said sweetly.

"Yeah, sure." Quintron returned to his conversation.

Not sure what to make of the fact that he was now
ignoring her, Kurala, feeling strangely subdued, quietly
left for her ship.

And high above
in the celestial heavens
an Angel looked down,
carefully observing her sister,
and sadly wept
by the light of the stars . . .

Chapter Fifteen:
THE HEALER

Upon her return to Galaxitron, Kurala and the two Maldon cowboys hurriedly met with Shakarr. First, they dispatched some pilots to Maldon. Then deciding that they needed a name for their combined forces, they settled on UNA which stood for Universal Nations Army. Kowtron and Textron were quickly dispatched to other planets where they could start training the UNA armies.

Kurala had much to catch up on. The most exciting news was that several healers had arrived in her absence. Shakarr had been hesitant to allow them to work on Shamo, although he had given them full access to the wounded spider warriors who were showing remarkable progress in recovering. There was one healer who was different than the rest, a strange woman named Neptha, and Shakarr had finally taken her to see Shamo. Apparently, he too, was getting better, although Shakarr himself hadn't had time of late to check in on him. He had heard that much of his pain was gone, although the Orion implants remained in position.

Listening with much interest, Kurala asked to meet with Neptha in her private quarters later that afternoon. For some reason she wasn't ready to see Shamo yet, wanting to meet with the healer first. So she busied herself by visiting the treasure piles and selecting many items to be moved into her quarters immediately.

Kurala spent the next several hours decorating her suite of rooms, and she had to admit, they looked much better after she was finished. She rewarded herself with a Vega wafer, carefully hoarding what she had left. Finally, there was a soft knock at her door. It must be the arrival of the healer.

Opening the door, she admitted a most unusual being. The woman was much younger than she, almost a girl actually. She was slight and pale with long blonde hair tied back in a loose braid. Her eyes were almost translucent and her entire being glowed with a golden transparency.

"Please come in and sit down. I am Kurala, Queen of Galaxitron and your name is Neptha, is it not?"

"Yes, I am Neptha El Ra," said the healer in a soft voice full of dancing light. She sat down on some silken cushions which were by the window.

Sitting nearby on identical pillows, Kurala stared at her with open interest. "Where do you come from, Neptha El Ra?"

"I come from the One. But I have spent most of my life as a captive on the planet Osannah. That is where your people found me and offered me my freedom if I came to Galaxitron to serve," Neptha said in her intriguing voice of rainbow music.

Kurala felt as if she could listen to her all day. There was much about this young woman which fascinated her. But, first she needed to learn about Shamo's condition.

"I have heard that you have been working with my husband Shamo. How is he progressing?" she asked.

"The pain is nearly gone, the implants are ready to be removed, but the problem intensifies," Neptha stated simply.

"What is this problem?" Kurala asked.

"That you must see for yourself. Shall we go visit him now? Then you shall learn the truth of his situation."

Nodding her ascent, Kurala arose and together the two women walked silently to Shamo's quarters. Passing the phalanx of bodyguards into his room, Kurala was astonished to discover that the curtains were open and sunlight was streaming everywhere! Shamo had always hated the light.

The King himself, was seated upon a small throne looking regal and important. He glanced up at Kurala as if she was a stranger. His wife was shocked at the detachment she felt from him. It was almost as if they had never met each other before.

Kurala tried to cover up this feeling of separation by greeting him warmly and rushing to his side. Shamo's eyes regarded her impassively. After a moment's hesitation, he spoke to her in a strange voice that sounded hollow.

"Oh, hel-lo. You must be my wife nam-ed Kur-al-a. Have you re-turned from where-ever you jour-neyed to? I guess that you must have, for you are stand-ing before me, aren't you?"

"Shamo, it is me! Whatever has happened to you?" Kurala cried out to him with anguish. She turned angrily to Neptha. "What have you done to him?" she yelled.

Neptha remained calm. "It is not my work, but the effect of the Orion implants. They are turning Shamo into an android. Can't you see that he is losing all his emotions, all his feelings of individuality?"

"Well, can't you remove these disgusting implants from him? What kind of healer are you?" Kurala was filled with a sense of appalling despair.

"Yes, I can remove them. I am one of the Master Healers. But, he will not permit me to take them out. I have tried to convince him to do so for weeks," Neptha replied with her musical tones.

Listening to her voice somewhat soothed Kurala.

She decided to try to approach Shamo again. "Please my beloved husband, please let Neptha remove your implants and make you whole once more!" she implored.

"No, I de-ny my per-miss-ion. Per-miss-ion de-nied. I am a ser-vant of the Dark Lords of O-ri-on. The OM-NI of O-ri-on are my mas-ters," Shamo intoned.

With desperation, Kurala turned to Neptha. "Can't we take them out without his permission? You can see that they are destroying him!"

"That I cannot do, for I cannot interfere with his free will, even to heal. At the time he received his implants, there was an agreement made. Usually this is given from false promises or partial knowledge. Often the person agreeing to receive implants is told that it will give them increased insight, more power or something else that they have been craving. Of course, after the implants are in, it doesn't matter anymore, since the truth of their being is so vastly distorted." Neptha El Ra gave Kurala a look filled with loving compassion. "Come, let us return to your quarters, if we may."

Kurala numbly let herself be led back to her rooms. Neptha asked if she wished to be alone.

"No, please stay, for once I don't want to be alone. I feel like crying and I never used to cry. I don't know what's wrong with me!" Kurala surprised herself because she had never spoken this openly to anyone before. Maybe Neptha was a witch and had enchanted the entire palace. This thought filled Kurala with suspicion.

"On the other hand, I prefer to be alone. Thank you for your time. You are dismissed." Kurala waved her arm towards the door with an imperious gesture. Neptha bowed and quickly left. After the door had closed and Neptha's footsteps died away, Kurala was suddenly overcome with shame at the manner in which she had treated the healer.

"What is happening to me?" she called out in desperation, then curling up on the floor cushions, she began to cry and cry until her body was racked with heartrending sobs. "Now, I'll never find out who I am. I'll never find my true people. And what am I going to do with Shamo as my enemy?"

Chapter Sixteen:
THE CONFEDERATION

Perhaps this would be an appropriate place to pause and discuss the matter of time. Most of this story is presented to you within the framework of what we term galactic time.

There are four main scales for measuring time within this dimensional universe. First there is earthly time which as we know it, is measured in 24 hour segments called days and 365 day segments which we call years. The second form of time is called galactic time. Here time stretches out; what was delineated as a month on earth is now more full of potentialities. Within a few months of galactic time, you can experience what on earth would take a year.

The third form of time within this dimensional universe is called celestial time wherein one year on earth equals one day in heaven. And concurrent with all other forms of time measurement, there is No-Time. In order to experience No-Time you must first anchor yourself into the Oneness of the Greater Reality. Inside No-Time, both time and duality cease to exist.

The same shift in measurement also applies to the concept of space and to the duration of life-spans. Within the galactic framework, embodiments last considerably longer than upon the earth patterning. Although distances are still measured by the speed of light, due to the capability of hyperspace, one is able to supersede the limitations of light speed. One also is given access to travel through the various chutes or *worm holes* within space.

The relative distance between space is further accelerated when you enter the celestial patterning. Distance is no longer measured by the speed of light. Traveling upon the starwaves, you are not only able to move through great distances at a rapid speed, but there are various control points and midway stations which enable one to move from point A to point Z instantaneously. Plus, one can easily shift dimensional realities by traveling through stargates.

In the Celestial Realms the duration of an embodiment as an individualized unit of consciousness is totally a matter of conscious free will. One is able to slip into and out of embodiment with ease, and can appear in several forms simultaneously.

Within No-Time, you are simply the omnipresent One and the Many.

Δ   Δ   Δ

Now we shall continue on with our story... Time has passed. The Maldon renegade fleet has successfully raided the Intergalactic Confederation's supply depot located on planet X432 in Vector 4. The newly acquired starships and arsenal of weaponry have been secreted away on various moons and satellites within Vector 5.

This has not passed unnoticed by the Intergalactic Confederation. Right now they are meeting within the Council of Arion in the star system of Arcturus. Although there were no survivors from the raid on their supply depot, a message was sent to them from one of their forces on X432 which reported the sighting of Maldon warships.

There is much discussion within the Council as to the reason behind the possible Maldon involvement. They have also pondered whether the Dark Lords of Orion are part of this attack. Panachar, Ashtar, Hokthor, Sentalaa, Zar, Hatonn & Soltec – many of the greatest of the Confederation's Star Commanders calmly discuss this breach of law. Throughout it all, there is one man who remains lost in deep thought. It is AAla-dar, silent because he has an intuition which keeps nudging at him that somehow Kurala is involved.

For the present it is decided that the Intergalactic Confederation shall be placed on full alert. Subtle inquiries will be made among those hidden ones in service to the Confederation. All supply depots shall be fully defended. Heavily armed garrisons will be placed in strategic locations.

Finally AAla-dar speaks, "May I request that doubled forces be placed along the key quadrants of both Vector 5 and Vector 6. I can't give you my reasons for this until I prove out my suspicions, but I feel it to be of extreme importance."

"Permission is granted, AAla-dar. It shall be placed into effect immediately," replied the leader of the Confederation.

"And I would ask to be relieved of all my duties for the present so I can do some exploration of this situation on my own," AAla-dar requested with unusual solemnity.

"Permission granted AAla-dar, for whatever you feel you must do. We would only ask you to notify the Council as soon as you discover anything of significance," said the leader.

"That shall be done," replied AAla-dar.

The meeting was soon over and AAla-dar departed rapidly for his private quarters. Although he originated from Aldebaron, he had no permanent home. Wherever he traveled, apartments were placed at his disposal. These were usually located in the spaceports, though on occasion, he actually stayed off the base. Such a case was Arion which was one of the planets of Arcturus. Actually, it was AAla-dar's favorite place to stay, for he was always given a beautiful, isolated pavilion on one of the myriad islands of this watery planet.

Arion was exquisitely beautiful, all azure blue sparkling oceans, cobalt islands, turquoise air. The islands were full of verdant plant life teeming with huge, tropical flowers. The pavilions and temples were composed of a translucent white substance, circular in design and open to the stars. Rain was unknown on fair Arion, but never was it needed for the air itself, was constantly moist and fragrant.

Quickly arriving at his island by a small hovercraft, AAla-dar entered his pavilion and was soon lost in thought.

"Kurala, it had to be her," he thought. "Who else would possibly do it? Who else would have the motivation?" He knew well several of the Maldon renegades and had served alongside Quintron during many battles. Quintron would not take on the Confederation by himself. But how had Kurala convinced him to aid her? And why did they need such a supply of weapons and a fleet of warships? Surely not merely to invade planets? Besides, Kurala hasn't conquered any planets outside of her Vector since I met her. What is she up to now?

Thinking so intensely of Kurala stirred up AAla-dar's emotions. He was still in love with her. He hadn't been able to forget her, though he had tried mightily. And he had always known that they would see each other again, although he had prayed that it would not be in battle as enemies. Why had that woman affected him so deeply? It was as if she had crawled right inside his skin. No matter where he went or what he was doing,

Kurala was always there with him. AAla-dar wondered if she felt the same way about him.

What didn't make sense at all was that if Kurala was still in alliance with the OMNI, why would she need to rob the Confederation's supply base? He knew with certainty that Quintron, as wild and unprincipled as he was, would never join forces with the Dark Lords. So what was his next step? Should he contact Quintron or Kurala? Who would be more likely to reveal the truth to him?

AAla-dar's heart solved this dilemma. For at the merest possibility of seeing Kurala again, it leapt within his chest. Also he was certain that Kurala would be unable to lie to him, even if she tried. Turning his attention to the best way to contact Kurala, he decided to send a message to her through one of their hidden ones asking her to meet him in a neutral zone, away from the spies of the OMNI. Possibly Mebsuta in Gemini would do just fine.

Chapter Seventeen:
THE MESSENGER

Inside the palace on Galaxitron, Kurala was pacing her suite of apartments. She had never given into pacing before, but she was now driven by a restless energy. Everything was happening too fast. The capture of the supply depot had been achieved smoothly, the troops were being trained into a precision fighting force and somehow, they were maintaining secrecy for they had not been visited by the Dark Lords for some time.

Shamo was still a problem. The more he returned to health, the greater a liability he became. Even Shakarr, as loyal as he was to Shamo, was beginning to see the disastrous results of the Orion implants which Shamo steadfastly refused to have removed. Kurala did not want to kill Shamo, but saw that she, or someone, might have to do something soon, before Shamo discovered what was really taking place on Galaxitron.

The worst thing that was happening to Kurala was her attacks of doubting when she questioned the direction of the course of destiny which she herself, had set into motion. During these moments, she often retired to her rooms and allowed herself to weep, sometimes for hours. After these bouts of crying had subsided, she was filled with shame and scorn at herself. Why she couldn't even trust herself anymore! If she wasn't sure of her purpose, then how could she expect anyone else to be? And how could they ever take on the dreaded OMNI without an invincible, united force?

Lost in her musings, it took several persistent knocks at her door before she heard them. Opening her door, Kurala was surprised to discover Neptha standing there expectantly. She had seen little of Neptha since the day of her return from Maldon. Although constantly intrigued by her, Kurala had been avoiding Neptha, simply because she didn't know what to make of her and didn't need any additional challenges right now.

"May I come in?" Neptha asked quietly.

Kurala had forgotten the dancing rainbow lights of Neptha's voice. It was so beautiful. "Yes, of course, please come in," she replied.

Closing the door firmly behind her, Neptha said, "I have an important message for you. If you promise never to ask me how I received this message, I will deliver it to you."

Masking her shock at Neptha's boldness, Kurala said in a voice full of imposing authority, "And what if I don't promise?"

"Then I shall willingly die before the message is delivered," said Neptha calmly.

And Kurala knew this to be the truth so she softened her manner and gave her promise. "But who is this message from?"

"From one who lives within your heart," said Neptha. "He wishes to meet with you about a matter of grave importance in a fortnight on Mebsuta in Gemini. He gives his word of honor promising you safe passage to and from this neutral zone."

"Surely this couldn't be from AAla-dar?" thought Kurala to herself. She asked Neptha, "How do I know who this message is really from?"

"He said that he would bring you all the Vega wafers you desire, unless you still prefer flies," said Neptha with amusement.

AAla-dar, it is from him! Kurala thought. "How did you receive this message, Neptha?" she asked.

"Remember your promise or there shall be no more messages," Neptha said, raising her hand in a gesture of warning.

"All right, forgive me for asking. I will honor my promise to you," said Kurala, surprising herself at her easy compliance. "Is there need for a reply?"

"You shall be there, will you not?" Neptha asked.

Without a moment's hesitation, Kurala answered, "Yes, I shall be there. Please tell him that I look forward to meeting him on Mebsuta."

"Thank you. I shall go now," said Neptha who quickly slipped out the door.

Kurala was completely stunned. She was filled with multitudes of unanswered questions. AAla-dar had sent her a message right to her very room! How could that be? And Neptha, who was she really? She couldn't be an evil witch if she received messages from AAla-dar. Was she one of the Confederation's spies? Kurala was going to have her watched even more closely. But only by someone she trusted, for she wanted Neptha to be able to still receive messages for her.

And what did AAla-dar want of her? Had he found out about her plans to fight the OMNI or was he just wanting to see her again? There had been something in the message about a matter of grave importance. Maybe he knew that she was behind the raid of the Confederation's supply depot? Well, whatever the reason, she was going to see AAla-dar in a fortnight and suddenly Kurala was filled with joy, the first glimpse of happiness she had experienced in a long time.

Chapter Eighteen:
THE DARK LORD

Lest you think that all these activities by Galaxitron and Maldon were passing unnoticed by the Dark Lords of Orion, let us set the record straight. One of the OMNI had known of these plans almost since the beginning. This was Zeon, the mysterious, handsome one who stood in the center of the dreaded Triad. Zeon differed from the other two, Triax and Narcron, in many ways. And it was he who held the final authority within the OMNI. Although he often stood back and let Triax and Narcron implement the Triad's actions, it was Zeon who held the knowledge and controlled the power.

Hence an intense rivalry and jealousy had manifested between Triax and Narcron towards Zeon. They tried to keep it unnoticed except amongst themselves where they secretly plotted against him as they awaited an opportunity to usurp his power. Their main complaint was that Zeon was not ruthless enough – if they were going to be Dark Lords they wanted to play it out with a terrible vengeance and wreck havoc and fear wherever they passed.

Alas, Triax and Narcron had lost themselves in their roles, like all of us have done time and again. But Zeon had not and this is what made him different from the rest. This was his mystery and his mark of greatness and why he was chosen to stand in the center of the OMNI. It could be said that if you truly looked at Zeon carefully, with your clearest vision, you would see a small sphere of white within his vast vortex of blackness. Only one being at a time within the entire forces of the Dark Lords of Orion was given this circle to embody. But it was essential to the Divine Plan in accordance with Universal Law, that always there be one in embodiment.

Zeon was fully aware of the continuous plots against him from Triax and Narcron, but their manipulations were so obvious that they were easily transmuted. As it was important that the OMNI presented an invincible, united front to the rest of the dimensional universe, he carried out no punishments against them, preferring to observe them quietly through the small white circle in his being which contained direct access to the All Seeing Eye.

It was through this opening that he had been watching Kurala. Knowing of her true origins in the Angelic realms, Zeon was highly amused by the direction she had chosen to pursue. "The Angelic Hosts must be thoroughly appalled by what Kurala is doing down here!" he thought to himself with amusement. But after his laughter subsided, he had a chilling insight. Knowing that there are no mistakes, *especially in heaven*, Zeon knew that somehow, Kurala's capture and embodiment on Galaxitron was serving some Higher Purpose. It was important that he remembered to pay attention to that, for he didn't want that Higher Purpose sneaking up on him unaware. After all, Kurala was about to declare war upon them! So the OMNI were playing a key part in this scenario as well.

It was funny though that this poor captured angel, married to a spider (!) on the impoverished planet of Galaxitron felt that she could take on the Dark Lords of

Orion! Zeon laughed heartedly, knowing full well that he could crush this ragtag force of deluded malcontents and spider people led by a fallen angel, any time that he chose to. But he was so vastly entertained by all these developments that he decided to let them continue with their plans without direct interference for as long as possible.

Unfortunately soon after this, X432, the Confederation's supply depot in Vector 4 was seized by unknown forces. This brought Triax and Narcron into awareness that something unusual was happening. The OMNI met in Council and placed their forces on full alert status. Zeon did not divulge that he knew who was responsible, for soon enough their spies would be reporting back to them. Several small squadrons of Dark Lords were assembled to make their presence felt in Vectors 3, 4, 5 and 6. They also renewed their defensive measures, anticipating possible reprisals from the Confederation, for the OMNI would probably be the leading suspects.

The Triad discussed at length whether or not they should send a message to the Intergalactic Confederation declaring their innocence in this matter. However it was decided that it served their purposes better to keep the Confederation in the dark, so they would not know who their real enemies were.

After Triax and Narcron left the Council chambers, Zeon turned his attention to further activating Shamo's implants. Then he waited and watched to see how destiny would play itself out.

Chapter Nineteen:
MEBSUTA

Several days before the fortnight had passed, AAladar arrived on Mebsuta. He wanted everything to be in readiness for his meeting with Kurala. Choosing the most luxurious of their guest suites, he had it fully stocked with Vega wafers plus a few other delicacies he thought she might like to try.

Although his heart was surging with emotion, AAladar refused to allow himself to indulge in any projections about Kurala's impending visit. Knowing her, it was impossible to determine how things might be between them. It was important that he focus on the task at hand, which was to prevent a cataclysmic war. AAla-dar was well aware that all the potentialities were at hand for the beginning of a major intergalactic war, the likes of which had not been seen for countless millenniums.

And he was certain that Kurala held the key. If he could get through to her, possibly the war could be averted before it had even begun. How ironic that he was also in love with this woman! That's probably why he was given this task of calling to the core of her Essence, doing whatever measures he could to return her to the light before it was too late for all of them.

Δ   Δ   Δ   Δ   Δ

During this time, Kurala was journeying to Mebsuta. She too, was engulfed with emotions, constantly pushing aside her expectations. Not knowing what to anticipate or even what AAla-dar wished to discuss with her, she finally refused to allow herself to think about it. Instead she concentrated on studying the various star charts she had been accumulating so that she could become more familiar with celestial navigation, knowing that this knowledge would be essential to her survival in the times to come.

These studies came easily to Kurala. It was as if she already knew the myriad star patternings and coordinants of the various vectors and simply needed to dust off her cellular memory banks. Sometimes, while concentrating on the key quadrants of vectors or the cosine frequencies surrounding null zone overlaps, Kurala would begin to remember traveling on the starry currents with a timeless ease. The funny thing was that she never felt herself to be within a starship; it was just she alone in her body, almost like flying. These reoccurring memories were so familiar!

Engrossed in her studies and experiences of remembrance, Kurala's journey passed by swiftly and without strain. As Mebsuta drew ever closer, she was swept along by a tide of rising excitement. Quickly changing into a stunning suit of red and purple with a long, narrow skirt, Kurala was ready to meet AAla-dar. *(She wanted badly to impress him with her newly discovered sophistication.)*

Glancing out the window at Mebsuta, she saw that the planet was covered with dense vegetation in lowland valleys out of which jutted high pointed rocky peaks. What a fascinating place! Then the futuristic spaceport came into sight – large spheres floating in the air and strange towers. Kurala had never seen anything like it.

AAla-dar watched the long awaited black ship with

the purple orchid land and felt a swelling inside his heart. Kurala had come! Standing alone outside the spaceport entrance, he waited impatiently for the hatch to open and Kurala to disembark. And suddenly, there she was, the woman of his dreams! AAla-dar wanted to run to her and sweep her up in his arms, but forced himself to wait until she approached. Kurala was even more beautiful than he remembered her; something had profoundly changed within her since he had seen her last. She no longer emanated cruelty and ruthlessness.

Kurala saw AAla-dar standing by himself at the doorway to the spaceport and was instantly filled with joy. He looked so familiar to her, as if she had been with him only yesterday. It was hard to believe that so much time had passed. Suppressing a smile, her being, nevertheless, glowed with delight.

There they stood, in front of each other now, gazing deeply into the other's eyes, not daring yet to speak. They both knew irrevocably, that the love between them had grown stronger still. Standing there in silence, their eyes drank thirstily from the chalice of their shared love. Not needing to touch or speak, they realized that somehow, they had become one.

Finally with a heavy sigh, AAla-dar spoke. "Kurala, you have come."

"Yes AAla-dar, I am here," Kurala replied, unable to withdraw her eyes from his.

"Shall we go inside?" he asked. Tossing her head in approval, she walked with him into the spaceport to their private accommodations.

Upon entering their suite, Kurala noted the exquisite luxury of the guest apartment. This time she did not attempt to mask her surprise. "Why, AAla-dar, this is simply stunning. I've never seen anyplace like it! This makes our gorgeous room on Deneb look dowdy. How do you find these places? I never knew such beauty existed."

"I'm glad you find it to your liking," said AAla-dar modestly, while greatly pleased that she was appreciative. He had thought that she would like Mebsuta. *('Just wait until she sees the island pavilions on Arion!' he thought to himself. He was saving those for later).* Then AAla-dar pulled Kurala into his arms and kissed her. They stood melting together for a long while, both of them basking in the glow of their long suppressed love.

Important as it was, the urgent business between them would have to wait. For the call of a rare, great love urged them to surrender fully, and this they did with total abandon. It was the only thing that either of them could do. All thoughts had been erased, all plans came to a total halt, the rest of the universe ceased to exist – nothing else mattered except being together, merging into one on level after level of their beings.

Three days passed by thus in No-Time. Days of few words, except the sweet murmurs of love. Days with no nourishment of food, even Vega wafers had been forgotten, for who needed physical food when the manna of purest love was available. Days and nights which blurred into oneness as the barriers between their separate beings dissolved away. Only bliss remained, bliss of a sublime quality they had never before perceived possible.

At last, they knew that they must return to galactic time, for there was much for them to do. With great tenderness, they drew apart, returning to their separate identities as much they could. Discovering a raging hunger, they spent over an hour eating Vega wafers and some of the other delicacies which AAla-dar had stocked. Finally they got down to the business at hand.

"Kurala, I know that you are responsible for the capture of our supply depot at X432 in Vector 4 and that you were aided by the Maldon renegades. What I don't know is how did you ever get Maldon to help you? They're a pretty rough bunch," AAla-dar began.

"It was quite easy, actually. I guess you could say that I impressed them with a combination of my navigation skills and my female charm." Kurala smiled with remembrance of her experiences on Maldon. "Quintron has a heart of mush under all his toughness." Then she shared with AAla-dar some of her experiences there. Both of them laughed so hard that they had tears running down their faces.

"Kurala, you are really something! Parts of you are unbelievably innocent. If you had any idea of what you are getting yourself into . . . Well if anyone could melt the hearts of the cowboys at Maldon, especially crusty old Commander Quintron, you're the one! But why did you want to seize our supply depot?" he asked with interest.

"We needed additional warships and weapons," Kurala answered calmly.

"Why do you need them? You haven't been invading planets lately," he said.

"Because I am declaring war on the Dark Lords of Orion." Kurala wasn't afraid to tell AAla-dar the truth. In fact, she was actually relieved that she could talk to someone whom she trusted. "We have been raising an army called UNA, Universal Nations Army, so we can finally become free of the OMNI's tyranny."

AAla-dar couldn't believe what he had just heard. "You are declaring war against the OMNI?" he stated incredulously. "Last time I saw you, you were proud to be working in alliance with them. What has happened?"

Kurala told him of her return to Galaxitron after their last meeting, how Shamo had received Orion implants and of her anger at the Dark Lords. This was followed by her visit to Maldon.

She continued, "The worst thing that happened was

during that night on my ship in Maldon while I was waiting for their decision. For the first time, I was seized by terrible doubts as to whether I should take on the Dark Lords. I even considered asking you for your help. But after Maldon decided to help me, I couldn't pull out."

"Oh Kurala, I wish you *had* contacted me; it would have been a lot simpler to handle back then. You know that I would have come and aided you. Commander Quintron and I go back a long way. We could have worked something out."

"Well, I didn't, for whatever reason. I have changed so much since I first met you that I don't even know who I am anymore. I can't even trust myself." Kurala almost began to cry, but hastily pulled herself together. She didn't want AAla-dar to see how weak and confused she had become. Next she told him of her return to Galaxitron, about the healer Neptha and how Shamo worsened and didn't recognize her anymore. Speaking of Neptha, reminded her of the message she had received from him. "Do you know Neptha El Ra? Is she one of the Confederation's spies?" she asked.

"I have never heard of Neptha. However, I did send the message to you. The way we do it isn't by sending messages to particular individuals, but rather by assigning them to a certain level of resonance where they are received by those attuned to that frequency," AAla-dar explained.

"Tell me Kurala, have you had any contact with the Dark Lords recently?" he asked.

"None. Somehow, they must not be aware of what we are doing," she said.

"That is not possible. The OMNI always know everything that is going on, especially within their own territories. For some reason, they must be choosing not to act," AAla-dar replied with certainty.

Kurala's heart filled briefly with ominous dread. "Well, it's just as well they haven't contacted us yet, since it gives us more time to prepare ourselves," she said courageously.

AAla-dar sat quietly lost in thought. How was he going to impress upon Kurala the gravity of their situation? Now that she had lost much of her lust for power and control, she emanated a beautiful innocence. He didn't want to destroy that, for along with her high spirited independence, it was the source of much of her strength. And she was going to need all her strength and courage in the times to come, no matter what course of action was followed. Yet, somehow she must be made to understand the full implications of what was going on.

"Let me attempt to explain to you what's happening," he began. "This is what has been put into play since our supply depot was seized. Right now the forces of the Intergalactic Confederation have been placed on full alert. Their fleets are positioning themselves along key quadrants in various sectors. They still don't know if the Dark Lords of Orion are involved, so it is likely that if they encounter any of the OMNI's forces, that battles may ensue."

AAla-dar continued, "We may also assume that the Dark Lords have been placed in full combat readiness and that their squadrons are being dispersed to various strategic positions. Since they are aware of the existence of a third force and the Confederation isn't, this places them in a position of superiority over the Intergalactic Confederation, upsetting the balance between dark and light within our entire universe. The reason why Galaxitron has not been attacked by now is probably because it serves the OMNI's purpose to keep the Confederation in the dark about the UNA forces."

He glanced at Kurala who listened attentively. "Then

there is the matter of Maldon which has never been known to engage in any actions except to achieve their own selfish concerns. Even though you may have charmed them, and I'm sure you did, don't ever fool yourself into thinking that you have the upper hand with them or that they have any sense of honor, because they don't. The reason that each of them was kicked out of the Confederation is because they were unable to follow higher authority. They're all a bunch of hardened outlaws who have no respect for anyone!"

"So what do you suggest that I do?" Kurala asked, finally seeing the implications of her actions.

"Before you decide what to do, I want you to be fully aware of where all of this is leading. Currently, there are three opposing forces of battle-ready fleets roaming around the skies all itching to fight. We are on the brink of a massive intergalactic war that can only be devastating to everyone! Something has to be done to diffuse this situation immediately." AAla-dar paused and took Kurala's hand. "I must serve the Confederation above all else, but I will aid you in any way that I can as long as it doesn't go against my vows to them."

"AAla-dar, if I removed my own forces from UNA, what would Maldon do? And what about the OMNI? Surely they will destroy our planet. Can your Confederation promise to protect Galaxitron?" she asked. Kurala couldn't believe that she was actually considering a shift in alignment to the Intergalactic Confederation! But,somehow, this made her feel greatly relieved, as if a gigantic burden was about to be removed from her.

This was the question he had been dreading to hear, for there was no easy answer to it. "Maldon would attempt to make reprisals on you, for they don't like being made fools of. Plus, now they'll be in trouble with the Dark Lords. Knowing Quintron, he'll probably try to make a trade with the OMNI, you for their freedom. The only place where you would be safe is deep within Confederation territory. Galaxitron itself, cannot be protected because it is located within the quadrants of the Dark Lords. Whatever way we look at it, your spider people are doomed unless they are evacuated immediately."

"AAla-dar, there is another possibility that you haven't looked at. What if UNA takes on the OMNI and wins? Then we could live peaceably alongside your Confederation and there would be no more strife in this universe," Kurala said with conviction.

"UNA cannot vanquish the Dark Lords. It simply isn't strong enough. You have captured one of our supply depots. Do you have any idea how many supply depots we have? And the Confederation itself with their vast resources, doesn't consider making war against the OMNI!" he replied.

"What if the Intergalactic Confederation came to the aid of UNA? Together we should be able to win," Kurala implored passionately.

AAla-dar had not thought of this option before. "Yes, united together, we might win. But I doubt that the Confederation would even consider it."

"But if they are the forces of light, don't they want to rid the universe of the forces of dark?" she asked.

"Yes, of course they do and we have battled with the Dark Lords for aeons. But neither of us ever wins the war, because it's impossible to win. We are in a universe of duality, Kurala. Within duality, one half of duality can never win. There is never a final, decisive battle, because just when you think the war is either lost or won, the pendulum swings back in the opposite direction. Fighting duality is like fighting with part of yourself, one hand hitting the other hand. It's frustrating and ultimately pointless."

"AAla-dar, isn't there some way we could get the Intergalactic Confederation to aid us? Would it help if I went to them? I'm not honorable like you are, but I can't just abandon Galaxitron. I know that it's an ugly, impoverished planet, but it's the only home I have."

As he was thinking of what effect a plea for help by Kurala would have upon the Confederation, a siren began to wail ominously throughout the building.

Kurala jumped up with surprise. "What is it, AAla-dar?"

"Full alert readiness, Alpha Code Frequency. This is serious!" He picked up the phone and pushed some buttons rapidly. "Commander AAla-dar reporting. Info please. . . Coordinates . . . Thanks." He clicked the coordinates into his pocket computer. Turning to her, he said, "Well Kurala, your war has already begun. UNA forces led by Quintron have engaged with a small contingent of the OMNI. I have to return to the Confederation immediately. O.K. my love, what are you going to do? Do you want to come with me?"

"You know that I want to be with you," Kurala said firmly. "But I can't leave my planet unprotected, not now, if the war has really begun. Please see if you can get the Confederation to help us."

"I'll do whatever I can, but don't count on us. And if you need me, try to send a message through Neptha. Remember that 1 will always love you, Kurala!" Grabbing his bag, AAla-dar gave her a quick kiss and was gone.

Chapter Twenty:
WAR BEGINS

I love you, AAla-dar!" Kurala cried out after him, but he was gone. She had better depart also. Hurriedly gathering up her things, she gave their beautiful guest quarters one last look of appreciation and rushed off to her ship.

Once aboard, Kurala gave orders for an immediate take off. Then she discovered that during her absence, several large crates of Vega wafers had been delivered. Now she was set; she would no longer have to eat insects! Setting the fastest course possible to return to Galaxitron, Kurala retired to her quarters.

She was furious at Commander Quintron. How dare he start fighting without consulting her! AAla-dar had been right; Quintron could not be trusted. How naive she had been, thinking that just because he responded to her charm, that she had control over him. No one ever would control Quintron. Actually, he was a lot like her and she would do well to remember that.

AAla-dar's departure had been so rapid and unexpected, that she hadn't begun to miss him yet. Thinking back to their long conversations, Kurala knew that he had spoken the truth to her. And she began to feel ashamed at all the trouble she had caused. But she was certain that she had made the correct decision in returning to Galaxitron, even if it led her into more danger, for she could not abandon her home not even for AAla-dar and the safety of his love. Maybe she was finally developing a sense of honor.

Lost in such thoughts, Kurala's journey homeward passed quickly. She pondered various courses of action upon her return. Of course, there was always the possibility that the Dark Lords would arrive there before she did and nothing would remain of Galaxitron by the time she got back. If only the Intergalactic Confederation would help them, there would be a much better chance of victory. Maybe she could come up with a scheme to trick the Confederation onto their side in the war. That was worth some thought.

Soon Galaxitron came into view. It was still intact. Communications with the skyport indicated that everything was fine. After landing, Kurala was met by Kowtron who handed her a message from Commander Quintron.

It stated succinctly:

"Hi baby! I was here, where were you?
Had something important to tell you,
but you weren't around.
Guess it's not important to you.
Am leaving Kowtron to help you.
By the way, had to off your husband.
Don't like getting involved with married ladies,
(just kidding),
but those implants were getting in the way.
  See you soon,
  Love, Q.
  P.S. The war has begun.

Kurala turned to Kowtron, "What does he mean by 'offing my husband?'"

"He killed the dude," Kowtron replied calmly.

"Quintron murdered Shamo?" Kurala asked incredulously.

"Yep, that's what I said," remarked Kowtron while gazing impassively at her with his big soft cow eyes.

"I don't believe it! Where's Shakarr?"

"You mean the old spider with the crippled legs? He's hiding in that slimy palace of yours," said Kowtron paying no attention to her anger. He apparently had no understanding as to why she was upset.

"I've got to see him right now. I'll meet with you later Kowtron!" Kurala said as she rushed off in one of their command modules.

Locating Shakarr was easy, Kurala knew that she would find him in Shamo's private quarters. There he was cowering in the corner racked with sobs.

"Shakarr, I just got back and heard about Shamo. What has happened?" she cried out with concern.

The old spider pulled himself back together with dignity. He was embarrassed that his Queen had discovered him in such a state, but truly, he felt that his heart was broken. "Commander Quintron arrived while you were gone. I don't like him at all; no one here likes him – he's just as mean as the OMNI. When you weren't here, he wanted to meet with Shamo. Well, Shamo started getting a lot worse right after you left. His Orion implants must have been activated or something. He became like a totally different personality, even talked in a different voice. Shamo didn't even recognize me anymore."

Here Shakarr paused to blow his nose noisily. "Shamo wanted to know everything, like where you had gone, what you had been doing, why we had so many more ships here? It was as if he had become a clone of the Dark Lords! Kurala it has been awful here!" Tears began to stream down Shakarr's cheeks.

"Shakarr, please be strong. We have much to do and

I really need your help. Try to tell me everything that happened," Kurala urged.

"Worst of all, Shamo was making plans to imprison you upon your return and was searching for the healer Neptha so he could torture her," Shakarr continued.

"Did he find her? Is Neptha all right?" Kurala wouldn't be able to bear it if anything had happened to Neptha. She was her lifeline to AAla-dar.

"No, I hid her away. But he was beginning to suspect me and I probably would have been the next to be tortured, except that's when that horrible Commander Quintron arrived with Kowtron. Now, Commander Kowtron's all right, he's a nice sort of fellow actually, although he looks kind of funny. I'm not used to cows you know; they make me nervous. But then, everything's been making me kind of nervous lately . . ." Shakarr was rambling on, getting increasingly incoherent.

"Shakarr, pull yourself together," Kurala commanded. "What happened after Quintron arrived?"

"Well, he sure wasn't happy that you weren't here. The Commander wanted to know where you had gone and what you were doing. But I told him that you hadn't told anyone. That made him really mad! He even searched through your apartments. Some of our guards were killed trying to stop him."

"Quintron went through my private quarters. How dare he!" Kurala was incensed at his lack of respect, although she knew that there was nothing incriminating for him to find. "What happened next, Shakarr?"

"After he was sure that you weren't hiding somewhere, he discovered Shamo. That was quite some meeting. They had a big confrontation, yelling at each other and all that, until suddenly Quintron blasted Shamo with a laser gun." Shakarr began to tremble, but continued on.

"After that, Quintron kind of took over the palace.

He was barking orders to everyone. We had no choice but to follow them. A few days ago he left, saying he'd be back real soon. Kowtron is still here, sort of his second-in-command, I guess. But he's not as mean, so things are kind of getting back to normal, as much as they ever will. I mean, what's normal anymore? Don't ask me. Shamo's dead and these weird people from Maldon running around all over our planet like they owned it." Shakarr was rambling again.

Kurala placed her hand upon Shakarr's head. "It's all right now. I'm back and we'll get everything straightened out. Don't worry anymore, Shakarr. I need you to find Neptha El Ra and bring her right away to my private quarters. Does either Kowtron or Quintron know about her?"

"No, they don't because she was hidden from Shamo when they arrived. I'll go get her right away." Shakarr bowed to his Queen and departed feeling greatly relieved that Kurala had returned.

Δ Δ Δ

Kurala went to her quarters and saw the mess that Quintron had left there. Her clothes were scattered all over the floor and it looked like he had slept in her bed. This made her furious and strengthened her resolve to get even with him. She decided to clean her room herself; she didn't want anyone else going through her things. This kept her quite busy for over an hour.

Soon enough, there was a soft knock on her door and Kurala let Neptha inside. She was overjoyed to see the healer. All her suspicions had melted away and Kurala felt that aside from Shakarr, Neptha was her truest ally on Galaxitron.

"Neptha El Ra, I am so happy to see you. I'm relieved that you are O.K.," she said warmly, holding out her hands to her.

Neptha gently took her hands and looked intently into Kurala's eyes. "I can see that your journey served you well," said she in musical tones.

"I'm going to get straight to the point, Neptha. We don't have much time. I don't know who you really are and maybe I never will, but I sense that you have a lot of knowledge which I don't. And I need your help for we're in a difficult situation here." Kurala shared with her all about the forces currently aligned for battle.

Listening attentively, Neptha showed immense concern for what was being said. When Kurala had finished, she replied, "I will help you in any way I can. We must find a way to bring peace back to this universe. However, it is important to remember that this situation is serving a Higher Purpose than we can presently imagine. When peace returns, we shall see that everything is vastly different; a transformation will have taken place. This entire situation signifies that it is time for a far reaching change that is going to alter the entire template of duality." Neptha paused for reflection, closing her eyes and going into a deep state of meditation. Kurala watched her with fascination.

After a few moments, Neptha reopened her eyes and continued, "Kurala, there is one thing you do not know about Galaxitron. Long ago, before the Shamo arrived on this planet, it was inhabited by some gentle beings called the Whispers. Many of the Whispers were destroyed by the Shamo when they conquered Galaxitron. Yet some of them remain here unseen by everyone except me."

"Where are these beings?" Kurala asked in astonishment.

"They are everywhere. Since their forms are nearly transparent, they can only be perceived as an iridescent sheen unless you have opened your Higher Sight," Neptha said.

119

"Can you show me one?" Kurala asked.

"I can only point out their rainbow lights until you develop your Sight, but I can also help you to do that, for it will greatly serve you in the times to come. Look over at your window, Kurala. Do you see any iridescence in the upper left hand corner?"

"Yes, I do! Is that a Whisper?" Kurala was truly amazed at this discovery. "Can you see its entire form?"

"Of course. They're very delicate in appearance, but exquisitely beautiful!"

Kurala laughed in delight. Suddenly there was a knock on her door. It was Shakarr, highly agitated and out of breath.

"Commander Quintron is landing at our space station!" he gasped. "What are we going to do?"

"We are going to remain calm, Shakarr. There is nothing to worry about. Tell him that I will meet him in our great hall shortly," she answered with authority. The old spider scurried off with the message, still huffing and puffing.

"Well Neptha, I had better get dressed to meet the Commander. Would you like to see Quintron? If so, we can meet with you in the Control Tower later," she said.

"Yes, I'll be there," Neptha replied.

Thus it was that a new alliance was formed, that of Kurala, Queen of Galaxitron and Neptha El Ra of the One. Little did Kurala know the full scope of the Higher Purpose they were truly serving.

Chapter Twenty One:
COMMANDER QUINTRON

Kurala sat calmly in the great hall until the approaching clatter of cowboy boots could be heard. She had donned a tight black lace jump suit to look more like a serious warrior. As he entered the hall, their eyes met in silent anticipation.

"Hey, baby, what a sight for sore eyes!" Quintron strode over to Kurala and kissed her passionately.

She pushed him away with haughty playfulness. "Quintron, what a surprise! Welcome to my planet of Galaxitron. What brings you here?" she asked.

The commander was a little put off by Kurala's aloofness. "Look lady, we've got a war going on and we've. . ."

Kurala cut him off sharply, "And why didn't you notify me before starting the war? It was my idea in the first place."

"I came here and you weren't around! Do you expect me to sit around waiting for you? By the way, where were you anyway?" he asked with rising irritation.

Ignoring his final question, Kurala retorted, "I certainly did not expect you to come to *my* planet and murder my husband!"

"Ah, come off it, that stupid spider whom you refer to as *your husband* was full of Orion implants! He was dangerous to have around. I did you a favor! And where did you go?" Quintron wasn't going to be put off from finding out what she had been up to.

"Commander, I don't ask for an accounting of every journey you take, and I expect you to show the same courtesy to me." She had better soften up; Quintron was getting extremely testy. "All right, I'll tell you where I was. I was simply on a little scouting mission. I wanted to see for myself how things were going at some of our UNA training camps. As this was a secret mission, I told no one where I was going."

"Yeah, then how come you went to Mebsuta in Gemini?" he drawled with suspicion.

Kurala masked her surprise while flashing Quintron a smile. "Because I was meeting surreptitiously with some Star Commanders who are fed up with the Confederation and might join us. I promised not to tell anyone, so don't ask me to reveal their names to you." This seemed to work. She took his arm and leaned against him seductively. "Now Quintron, let's get to work on our plan of battle, shall we?"

The Commander knew that Kurala was playing a game with him which made him even madder, yet she was also damned exciting. He began moving his hands all over her body, desiring this woman as he had no other.

"Uh, excuse me Commander . . ." Kowtron stood in the doorway looking at them with his large cow eyes emanating an air of solemnity. "Uh, Quintron, I think that you're needed at the Control Tower. Enemy ships are coming. I think that they're from Orion, the Dark Lords that is."

Swearing silently to himself, Quintron said, "Well come on baby, maybe the OMNI are paying you a visit."

The three of them hurried to the Control Tower. Sure enough, three OMNI warships were rapidly approaching. There followed a quick discussion as to what they should do. Kurala thought that they should let them land and see what they wanted. Overriding her suggestion, Quintron quickly gave orders for UNA ships to engage them in battle. Within seconds, six UNA warships were deployed to divert them from Galaxitron. The ploy worked, for the three OMNI ships altered their course and raced after the aggressive UNA forces.

While they were watching this drama through the large windows of the Control Tower, there was a massive explosion which rattled the windows and shook the building.

"What was that?" Kurala cried.

"A ship was destroyed," Kowtron replied dryly. Two more explosions followed in rapid succession. "There's two more gone. I wonder whose ships they were?"

From the radar control came the report, "Two UNA ships destroyed and one Orion."

"Not bad, for a beginning," said Quintron. "Wait until they hit us with a real squadron. These were probably just messengers."

"We just attacked their messengers?" Kurala asked incredulously.

"Yep, that way we don't have to be bothered with replying," Quintron replied with amusement. "Hey, lady, don't you know anything about war?"

"Of course, I do," Kurala retorted, "but I thought that everyone had agreed to give messengers free right of passage."

"Well, we're not everyone! We never said that the Trons were honorable, at least not in the normal sense of the word. But we do get the job done; that you can count on."

"The other two OMNI ships have departed," reported the radar control.

"Well, we got off easy, for now," Quintron said. "We better get away from here and into some real action before they decide to attack. I'll go ready our forces."

Kurala was numb with shock. It had finally sunken

in that war had begun. Yes, this terrible, impossible war that she was responsible for starting was already claiming its victims. And she had probably doomed Galaxitron in the process. She gazed about the room wildly, looking for something to steady her, to bring her back into a position of control, for Quintron had surely seized that from her. Then her eyes came upon Neptha El Ra sitting quietly in the corner.

Quickly, Kurala ran to her side and whispered, "Neptha, what should I do?"

"You have to go to war Kurala, but while you are out there, try to be a voice of reason. Whenever you can, insert integrity into the situation. Always look for a graceful solution, a peaceful way to end the war. Try to get the Confederation to aid you. With them on your side, you might be able to negotiate a truce with the OMNI." Neptha spoke quietly with music dancing in her words.

"Neptha, would you come with me?" Kurala asked.

"No, I shall stay here with the Whispers. But deploy as many of the spider people as you can. They shall be far safer in space. After they are gone, I can employ a forcefield of protection on Galaxitron, making it appear invisible. Whenever you need my help, just visualize me standing before you, and I shall be there."

Kurala nodded in silent agreement.

"One other thing," Neptha added, " Quintron is not to be trusted. He has his own agenda to achieve, which is quite different than yours. The Maldon forces will fight with you for as long as it serves their purpose, after that, you had better watch out. However, in the end Quintron will render you a great service, simply out of his love for you, which is real." Neptha reached up and embraced Kurala. "Go now and play out this horrible war with the fullest of your abilities; I will see you again when this cycle is nearly complete."

Fighting back her tears, Kurala ran from the tower.

And high above
in the celestial vastness
an angel looked down,
carefully observing her sister,
and sadly wept
by the light of the stars . . .

Chapter Twenty Two:
THE COUNCIL OF LIGHT

The secret meeting had been in session for many days now. It was a most rare gathering, for never before had the Intergalactic Confederation petitioned the Council of Light for advice on a matter that they could have decided upon on their own. But this time, the stakes were so huge, the Confederation felt that they needed Higher Guidance before they acted.

As this matter was slowly pondered by the Council, the deliberations continuously dissolved into lengthy silences making the representatives of the Confederation become increasingly impatient. They knew full well that a course of action had to be decided upon soon.

Triple Commander AAla-dar sat among them, paying close attention to the slightest nuance. He had already presented his information as to the involvement of both Kurala and Maldon. Impartially he had imparted Kurala's plea for the Confederation's help. All of this had met with a thoughtful silence. The meeting continued on thus for several more days, until one evening as they adjourned for the night, Uriel-la who was officiating for the Council of Light, announced that the Council's advice would be revealed in the morning.

The Intergalactic Confederation filed out slowly, relieved that the time of decision was soon approaching. The Council remained in session. A deep, all pervading silence descended upon the Council's chambers. For several hours it was so. The only sound which could be heard was of one unified breath, endlessly repeating itself.

△ △ △

Now, from the silence, a voice could be heard. "I am El-o-wa," it began. The being stood and silently did its mudra before the others. "If the Intergalactic Confederation lends their support to the OMNI against the UNA forces, perhaps this will bring the war to swift completion." El-o-wa sat down while another shining being stood doing its mudra.

"I am Mitra-An. If the Confederation combines with the OMNI to defeat the rebel UNA forces, what will be different? We shall still be imbedded in duality."

"I am Ama-Ra Antares. Yet, if the Confederation aids UNA, their combined forces could possibly defeat the Dark Lords. And is not our task to hold in balance the template of duality in this dimensional universe?"

Another stood and gracefully did its mudra. "I am Solanel. Truly, we have long awaited the evolution beyond duality. But is it now the time? Have we received a sign that this is so? Are the members of the Council of Orion ready to remove their robes?"

△ △ △

Once again, the entire Council lapsed into silence for several hours. This time they journeyed to the horseshoe shaped Council of Orion which was located in the zone of overlap within the area of the belt. Sitting on the left hand side were those wearing the black robes while on the right side were the ones in white.

At first it looked like nothing had changed. Each side appeared to be rooted into their position, believing themselves to be right and the others wrong. They still perceived their side as being separate from the other. Duality reigned supreme as it had ever since the creation of the original template of this Great Central Sun System. Arguments ranged back and forth between the light and dark robed ones as they tried to convince their opposites to see things their way.

Suddenly the Council of Orion began to dim. A brilliant radiance was superimposed upon the scene. The shining Presence of Lord Metatron, overseer of the zone of overlap came into view. He smiled warmly at the observers from the Council of Light.

"So, to your eyes, everything appears the same as before within the Council of Orion, does it?" Metatron spoke. "Then I would ask you to look closer, go deeper into the scene which is before you. See beyond what is readily visible."

Metatron faded from view and the Orion Council returned stronger and clearer than before. The Council of Light gazed deeper, noticing myriad small details they had missed the first time. Yes, a few of the robed ones of Orion were actually listening to what the other side said. There were jokes which were laughed at by both sides. It appeared as if a sort of mutual rapport was developing. It was subtle, for sure, but it had never before been apparent.

The voice of Lord Metatron rang throughout the heavens, "Possibly they are waiting for a sign or an event which will unify them into their inherent Oneness? I shall show you the key."

Next a searing triangle of shining, magenta light flashed before them. All else disappeared into dark-

128

ness. The magenta triangle shimmered with magnificence for a moment of No-Time, then an amazing thing happened. In an instant, it became smaller and smaller until with a whooshing sound it imprinted itself within the cellular memory banks of each member of the Council of Light.

Δ Δ Δ

Finally within the chambers of the Council of Light, a being stood and shared its mudra. "I am Ra-El-Ra, the Keeper of the Flame. The Council of Orion is nearly ready. The rising of this third force called UNA signifies that the time of completion is approaching. We must be very correct in the course of action we choose."

"I am Uriel-la. And what if we do nothing? Possibly that is the best course of action. Then we shall not interfere with destiny."

"I am Mikael-An. If we do nothing, then UNA will be destroyed by the OMNI and we are back where we started. Nothing will be accomplished. There is a great lesson in this for us."

More silence descended upon the Council of Light while each member tuned into the One, seeking clarity and impeccability of Purpose. . .

Δ Δ Δ

Slowly a shining one arose and did its mudra with deep concentration. "I am Zalador. **The keyword is triangulation.** In order to move beyond duality, we must complete it. This is done by creating a third point which changes duality's form into a triangle. The triangle opens the doorway!" Zalador sat down flushed with radiance.

"I am An-Ta-Ra Solar. If the Confederation enters the war as a third force, battling equally with the OMNI and UNA, it will be able to achieve the desired state of triangulation. This has the potential of shifting the patterning. Lord Metatron has given us the key to completing duality!"

The entire Council Chambers hummed with mounting excitement. This was no ordinary matter which lay before them. It was the long prophesied shift to a new spiral patterning beyond duality! The time had finally come. Messengers were rapidly sent to call forth the representatives of the Intergalactic Confederation who quickly assembled in a state of heightened anticipation.

Uriel-la stood and did her mudra before the Council. "I am Uriel-la," she stated in clear tones. "We have pondered well the question which you have put before us. Here is our advice to you. Enter this intergalactic war with your fullest might. Take neither the OMNI nor the UNA forces to be your ally, instead make battles with whomever you encounter. Know well that this truly serves your Higher Purpose and the evolution of this entire dimensional universe."

The Confederation members listened with a stunned silence. Surely the Council of Light wasn't urging them to battle two foes at once. That could easily destroy the entire Intergalactic Confederation. And what was this Higher Purpose of which they spoke?

Uriel-la continued as if reading their collective thoughts, "We cannot speak of the nature of our Higher Purpose at this time. But it is of vast importance to everyone within this universe. There is something of primary significance which we must stress. You must be very careful not to injure any of the leaders of either the OMNI or the UNA forces. If it becomes necessary, you are to intercede and protect them with all the power at your disposal. It is important that they continue on in order to play out their chosen roles within this vast drama."

Now the Confederation was truly confused. They were to take on both the OMNI and UNA, but not to kill their leaders. That was their best chance at survival.

"We know that you have many unresolved questions about what we have advised," Uriel-la said, "but we are unable to answer them at this time. Please, trust the integrity of our vision; we have not let you down before. And know that by doing this, you do all of us a great service. We cannot aid you with strategies of war, besides that is not necessary as you are the most skilled warriors within this universe. The task which we have set before you may appear formidable, but it is important to remember that it is in total alignment with the Higher Purpose. Thus you shall be continually aided from On High."

Adjourning the meeting, the Council of Light filed out in joyous exaltation, knowing that their work was nearly complete. The representatives of the Intergalactic Confederation remained in their seats for several minutes longer, wrestling with emotions of shock, betrayal, abandonment, fear, disbelief and even anger. AAla-dar sat in stunned submission; he could not believe what they had been told to do. The vows of the Intergalactic Confederation to serve the Higher Purpose beyond all else were tested beyond all previous limits.

Thus it was that the mighty Intergalactic Confederation did lend its fullest support to fight in the impending war for supremacy and control of this dimensional universe. The Council of Light had chosen wisely, for truly triangulation is the key to freedom.

Chapter Twenty Three:
THE BATTLES ESCALATE

To spare you some of the pain of remembrance, we shall leap ahead in time. However, before we continue on with our story, it must be noted that all of us took part in this horrible intergalactic war. Each of us has locked away within ourself, the memories of what we saw and what we did. Our experiences in this war have affected our entire cycle of embodiments on Earth. So great was our guilt and shame, that we have buried our tragic memories under layers of forgetfulness. And because of these repressed memories, we have constantly been afraid of our power. We have developed issues around the areas of denial, fear, trust and separation that must now be healed.

While Kurala's story is but a fragment of the whole, it is presented to you that you may step through the doorway of remembrance in order to free you for the times ahead . . .

Please allow yourself to remember your own part in this history and forgive yourself and all others. Release the dammed up memories and step forward into freedom . . .

△ △ △ △ △

For several terrible years now the battles have raged throughout the myriad galaxies. Few of the star systems located outside of the territorial quadrants of the OMNI and the Intergalactic Confederation have been untouched by war. But now the battles have spread inside these long respected boundaries. This horrific conflagration has killed billions of beings and destroyed nearly a million planets. All three of the opposing forces have been severely depleted. The entire universe is engaged in the war effort to some degree. Whole solar systems have been blown up in the elusive struggle for a final victory. And still the flames of war burn on unchecked. . .

Triple Commander AAla-dar fights with his fullest concentration. He has grown weary of war, not wanting to ever engage an enemy warship in battle again. His eyes are filled with a deepening sadness that was not present before, for he has seen far too much. Memories of close comrades in arms, those who served with dedication, being blown to bits of dust, flood through his heavy heart. Yet he continues on with courage and daring, for the need is always greater than before.

AAla-dar has not forgotten Kurala and loves her still. He has long anticipated the moment when he will discover her in the midst of the confusion of battle, but her presence has ever eluded him. He is certain that she must be surviving this terrible carnage, for otherwise he would hear reports of her death. Instead there are wild stories of her exploits which become evermore fanciful. But there is no time for romantic musings, only destruction, cleverness and focused flying. He wonders at the irony of falling in love with the woman who began this war which is ravaging not only his honored Intergalactic Confederation, but the entire universe.

And will anyone survive this? AAla-dar pushes that thought aside like an unruly weed, for he must not lose his faith. Did not the Council of Light promise them that this war was serving the Higher Purpose of all? The

Council has been keeping pretty silent of late. Well, they had better not have made a mistake. . .

Returning to the commander's quarters of his ship AAla-dar sets course for the Star System of Rastaban in Draco, territory long controlled by the Dark Lords – heading right into a sector of the heart of darkness.

Δ

The Queen of Galaxitron has now become a seasoned warrior. Her expertise at the controls of her ship have earned her the honorary title of Triple Commander for she is acknowledged by all of her foes as one of the best. Kurala has become somewhat of a legend, for none have been able to capture the elusive black warship emblazoned with a purple orchid. There is much conjecture as to how this unknown woman managed to obtain her skill and training. In Kurala's case we would have to say that she came by her talents in battle naturally, without schooling. The required knowledge appeared to be imbedded within her cells and came forth whenever needed.

Of course, she carried the secret of her communications with Neptha El Ra, which served her greatly in times of confusion or impending disaster. Neptha always seemed to know exactly what she should do. And Kurala followed Neptha's advice without question. Galaxitron itself has been spared the grief of war, for through Neptha's magic, it had disappeared from sight and even the OMNI could not find it. All of the Shamo had been evacuated from the planet and it is inhabited once again by the gentle Whispers who are transforming it back into a peaceful place of shimmering music and dancing rainbow lights.

As for Kurala herself, she is neither happy nor sad. There is no time for either. She simply continues on day by day, trying to see this war through to its appointed conclusion. Ceasing to hate the OMNI, ceasing to despair whenever she must blow up starships belonging to the Confederation, Kurala goes through the motions of war surfeit of emotions, searching only for a way out, for a doorway to open into a peaceful resolution.

And yes, sometimes her heart flutters to life when she spies a new Confederation squadron approaching, thinking perhaps that AAla-dar will be there. And then, what will she do? She has received no word from him since this war began. Constantly she asks Neptha if there are any messages for her. Neptha's answer is always the same, but the healer reassures Kurala that AAla-dar lives. "Maybe AAla-dar blames me for starting this war with my blind arrogance," she thinks. But within her heart, Kurala knows that AAla-dar loves her truly. She is torn between wanting desperately to see him and praying not to encounter AAla-dar in battle.

Aboard her ship is the old spider Shakarr, terrified beyond his wits, yet still bound by his loyalty to serve her until the end. He shakes and mutters incoherently more than ever, but Kurala patiently reassures him that all will be well. Many other spider people have joined her wing of the UNA fleet for few of them wanted to go off with Commander Quintron.

Quintron himself, is off on his own in a distant quadrant with a large group of the UNA forces. They are doing well, according to the reports which Kurala receives, although it seems as if they are attacking the Confederation more heavily than the OMNI. The Maldon Cowboys probably have a bit of a personal vendetta against the Confederation for kicking them out, Kurala realizes with dismay. Hence she sends Quintron a forceful message reminding him that their war is against the Dark Lords, not the Confederation!

Another splinter group of the UNA forces led by Commander Kowtron has recently aligned with Kurala's squadron. For several weeks, Kowtron stayed aboard Kurala's ship in order to visit, and a genuine sense of fondness has grown between the two leaders. Kowtron exhibits a simple kindness which often touches Kurala. He is not as ruthless as the other Trons. Kurala has looked deeply into his soft, cow-like eyes and seen a concern for the ravages of war. She has noticed that often he will show mercy to those whom they vanquish when the other warriors from Maldon would not.

Now Kowtron has returned to his own ship and together they have decided to attack the OMNI's heavily fortified outpost of Rastaban in Draco. Moving rapidly through hyperspace, they prepare for a surprise attack.

Chapter Twenty Four:
RASTABAN

FORWARD THRUSTS SCREAMING – SURGING AHEAD – STRAINING UNDER THE PRESSURE OF TOO MANY MEGAVOLTS OF ACCELERATION :

The UNA forces arrive in the airstream above Rastaban – showering the star system with photon vapors, laser jets and implosion bombs. The skies are filled with attacking warships. Instantly, Rastaban retaliates by sending forth terrifying death rays of a hideous, neon red which dematerialize everything they encounter. The deadly red beams sweep back and forth across the sky like searchlights. In the first fifteen minutes, a fifth of the UNA fleet is caught by surprise in the red beams and disappears forever. They have simply ceased to be.

Kurala winces at the sudden loss of so many of her people, yet at the same time, strengthens her resolve. With blindingly rapid maneuvers she dodges the deadly red beams and sets loose samples of her entire arsenal of weapons upon the Rastaban System. Next UNA is confronted with a vast fleet of OMNI warships zooming toward them, shooting green lasers.

"This battle is more than we had anticipated," Kurala thought. "It just might be our final one. Well, we might as well go out giving it everything we've got!"

On it went, for hours and hours, for days upon days, each opposing fleet becoming increasingly smaller and weaker. Many of Rastaban's planets had now been blown up. The air was filled with strangely shaped chunks of asteroids and moons. Huge fires raged out of control on the planets remaining. Then the balance suddenly shifted against UNA as reinforcements for the Dark Lords began to arrive. These new fleets were fresh and fully equipped. They were lusting for battle.

Kurala began to lose hope. In desperation she called upon Neptha. "Neptha, I fear we have met our end. Can you help us?"

Neptha instantly appeared before her, although her presence was unseen by anyone else.

"Help has already arrived, look behind you off to your right," Neptha quickly replied. "It is a fleet of the Intergalactic Confederation under the command of one you know well."

"AAla-dar? Is it really him?" Kurala asked with disbelief. As she glanced out her window she saw a large squadron of the Confederation bearing up on their right. This renewed her sense of hope and she returned to the surging battle with new energy and clarity.

As they approached the ensuing chaos of battle, AAla-dar quickly sized up the situation. UNA was getting wiped out by the OMNI. So he gave rapid orders for the Confederation ships to aid UNA in this lopsided battle. It was only after they had fully engaged their forces to defend UNA that he noticed the long sought after black warship with the purple orchid! "Kurala is here; I must protect her whatever the cost," AAla-dar vowed to himself.

With the help of AAla-dar's forces, the battle esca-
lated. All the swirling, churning warships tried to dodge
the penetrating red beams from Rastaban, but it was
not always possible. Even many of the OMNI ships were
dematerialized from being trapped in the wrong place at
the wrong time.

Throughout the following days as the war for
Rastaban continued to its fateful conclusion, Kurala
tried to keep the Confederation's command ship in
sight. Observing AAla-dar's daring maneuvers, she was
alternately filled with anxiety or thrilled at his brilliant
technique. He was the most magnificent Star Commander she had ever encountered, infinitely better
than her, she readily admitted. Of course, he had much
more experience than she did.

AAla-dar too was greatly impressed with Kurala's
battle prowess. As a brilliant commander, she was
nearly his equal. In the midst of fighting one of the most
dangerous battles of his life, he constantly kept her
position pinpointed, so he would be ready to assist her
if needed. He was deeply grateful that they did not find
themselves to be enemies in their first encounter in the
skies.

At last after weeks of devastation, the fight was
winding down. The OMNI forces were still putting up a
half hearted resistance, but they knew the battle had
been lost. OMNI warships could be seen slowly retreat-
ing one by one. Each day, less of them were present.

AAla-dar moved his ship closer towards Kurala in
order to catch a glimpse of her through the windows.
She watched him come nearer with rising excitement
for she yearned to see him too. As their ships were
approaching closer together, and as their attention was
fully focused on finally seeing the other – it came as a
total surprise when suddenly the warship of Com-

mander Kowtron zoomed towards AAla-dar in attack mode, engines screaming, laser rays fully activated!

"Oh no!" Kurala screamed. Without a second's hesitation, without any forethought, she blasted Kowtron's ship with a photon beam. It vaporized within moments.

In the instant before total vaporization, as it was turning transparent, Kurala recognized Kowtron's insignia on the ship she had just destroyed.

"No, no! What have I done?" Kurala was filled with despair for she had truly loved Kowtron. Why had he attacked AAla-dar? Was it to protect her or because he too, like the other Trons still held grudges against the Confederation? This she would never know.

Throwing her ship into full reverse she gave the signal for the entire UNA fleet to retreat. Shaking with sobs, Kurala shoved the controls into hyperspace, moving them as far away as possible from Rastaban. Then she ran to her quarters to cry and cry as if her heart was truly breaking.

Chapter Twenty Five:
REVENGE

When Commander Quintron heard of Kowtron's death at the hands of Kurala, he was furious. Kowtron had been Quintron's best friend and had been responsible for saving his life innumerable times. Why had that stupid woman killed him? He couldn't bear to dwell on the fact that Kowtron had been vaporized, for that was one of the worst deaths possible. Quintron found it impossible to forgive Kurala for what she had done. He didn't even care to hear her reasons behind it. There was simply no excuse that would be acceptable to him.

For sometime, Quintron and his UNA fleet had been in the constellation of Eridanus, skirmishing with the Intergalactic Confederation, trying to find an opening to invade their stronghold of Acamar. He hadn't been meeting with great success since Acamar was one of the Confederation's main garrisons and was strongly fortified.

To get his mind off his lack of success in conquering Acamar, Quintron focused on how he would get even with Kurala. He had to do something to show that bitch that she couldn't mess around with the Trons of Maldon. Besides, he didn't like the way she was always leading him on and putting him off. Deciding upon a plan of action gave him a slight sense of satisfaction. Occasionally Quintron would experience a twinge of remorse, but the memory of Kowtron, his greatest buddy ever, strengthened his resolve.

Thus it was that Commander Quintron sent an urgent summons for Kurala to meet with him at the star system of Reticulum, not far from Acamar. The message was worded in his own, inimitable style:

> Hey, baby!
> How're you doin'?
> This war is getting stale fast.
> Think we better get together soon.
> Meet you in Reticulum, Vector 2,
> star system Zeta
> on the red and grey planet.
> Right away.
> Very important.
> You better be there or else (just kidding).
> Love ya babe, Q.
> P.S. If you don't show, I'll come after you.

Now he had best get to work for there was a bit of planning necessary for this encounter with Kurala. Quintron scribbled another hasty message and sent it off immediately. Chuckling to himself, he was well pleased with how easily he had set into motion such a dramatic form of revenge. And maybe it could even end this boring war!

Δ

When Kurala received Quintron's message, she felt a cold shaft of impending dread penetrate her body. Whatever this meeting was about, it was most likely not going to be pleasant.

"This doesn't sound good. I don't think that I'll be able to charm my way out of this one," she remarked to Shakarr who stood by her side trembling more than usual.

"Kurala, I don't think we should go meet with Quintron. Isn't there somewhere we could go hide? Maybe we could just hang out on some little moon or piece of asteroid and he won't be able to find us," Shakarr stammered. "That Quintron is a real mean sort and now that Kowtron's gone, we don't have anyone to protect us." His face was covered with tears; poor Shakarr was so terrified, he was blubbering like a baby.

"My dear Shakarr, there is no place where we could hide from Commander Quintron. If he really wants to find us, he will," Kurala replied wearily. "And it will be a lot worse for us if we don't go to meet him willingly. Set course for Reticulum in Vector 2," she ordered. "Shakarr, please don't worry anymore. We've been protected thus far. I'm going to my quarters now for some rest, so take care of things for me on the bridge, will you?" She hugged Shakarr tightly and departed.

In the privacy of her own quarters, Kurala began to feel uneasy. She had known that there would be a showdown with Quintron ever since Kowtron's terrible vaporization at Rastaban. Someone like Quintron wouldn't take the death of his best friend lightly. And of course, he wouldn't be thrilled if he found out that she had killed Kowtron while saving the life of the man she loved – who just happened to be from the Intergalactic Confederation! No, this impending meeting at Reticulum was not going to be easy or fun.

Kurala herself was still beset with sorrow at the memories of Rastaban. "Why did it have to be sweet, silly Kowtron that attacked AAla-dar?" she wondered with dismay. All that she and AAla-dar had wanted was just a glimpse of the other. That's all, no stolen kisses or days in No-Time, nothing grand or extravagant – simply a glimpse of their beloved. And look at the ramifications it had wrought!

Ever since that fated day, she had avoided the myriad battles of this crazy intergalactic war. Kurala

143

had sent off her fleet to continue the fight while her own ship had been in constant motion, traveling from one galaxy to the next, keeping as far away from the action as she could. And still the pain and sleeplessness did not go away. Still she could not forget.

She was immeasurably weary of the ravages of war, cursing herself for bringing it to birth. "Well, I probably deserve whatever punishment Quintron has in store for me," Kurala thought bitterly. "Maybe it will serve to numb my pain. Better yet, perhaps even Quintron is getting tired of battle; he did mention something about 'the war getting stale.' I wonder if at our meeting, I could persuade him to end the war?"

It had been a long time since she had called upon Neptha for advice since Neptha never came to her unbidden. This felt like an appropriate time to do so. The healer appeared instantly, gazing at Kurala with sparkling eyes. Neptha was becoming more beautiful and ethereal each time that Kurala saw her. Life on Galaxitron with the Whispers must be agreeing with her.

"Neptha, you probably know that we are on our way to Reticulum to meet Quintron. Do you have any advice for me?" Kurala asked. "Is it wise for us to go there?"

"It is not a question of whether or not it is wise to go to Reticulum," Neptha replied. "You have already chosen to make this journey."

"What is going to happen when we get there?" said Kurala.

"I'm not allowed to reveal that to you," Neptha responded. "However, I can state that whatever happens will be serving the Higher Purpose of all. It is important for you to remember that, even if the situation appears bleak for a time. That's all I can tell you."

"Please Neptha, can you help me?" Kurala implored.

"Always remember that I am with you, as is the love of your Star Commander AAla-dar," Neptha said with a lilting resonance which soothed Kurala for a few moments.

After the healer's image faded away, Kurala no longer felt as reassured as she would have liked. Even Neptha wouldn't tell her what to expect. Undoubtedly some terrible surprise awaited her on Reticulum and she was going to have to face it all alone.

And high above
in the celestial heavens
an Angel looked down
upon her sister
and prepared herself
to descend into matter
by the light of the stars . . .

Chapter Twenty Six:
RETICULUM

Finding Zeta, the brightest star in Reticulum was easy after Kurala had located the constellation in Vector 2 on her star maps. Reticulum was also known as *The Net.* And Kurala smiled at Quintron's clever lack of subtlety, for she knew without a doubt that a trap had been set for her. Maybe she was simply too tired, but nothing seemed to matter anymore. If Quintron wanted to capture or double-cross her, even if he was plotting to kill her, Kurala no longer cared. Perhaps, it would serve the purpose of ending this horrible war. Almost anything would be worth that.

On the journey to Reticulum, Kurala took the time to reflect back on her life, that is, what she could remember of it. She regretted that she had been unable to get Shamo to reveal her past history. Surely he must have known where she had originated from and who were her true people. Then she had an amazing flash of inspiration. It was so obvious that Kurala couldn't believe that she had never thought of it before. Quickly sending a summons for Shakarr to come to her quarters, Kurala waited in nervous anticipation.

The old spider arrived huffing and puffing, but devoted as always.

"Shakarr, please sit down and make yourself comfortable. I need to talk with you and this may be our last opportunity," she began.

Trembling with fear, Shakarr sat before her. "What is it, your Highness?"

"You are one of the very oldest of the spider people. You knew Shamo for a long, long time, did you not?" Kurala questioned him gently.

"Yes, I was with him since the beginning ever since our emergence from the underground fissure." Shakarr began to grow teary at the mention of the spider king.

"I know that we have never talked about this before, but it is very important that you share with me all that you can. Shakarr, do you remember when I first came to Galaxitron?" she asked very softly, almost afraid to breathe, lest it startle Shakarr into not answering.

"Of course I do, I was there. I remember everything. I even helped tie you up with those big black sticky ropes we used to use," Shakarr replied.

"And could you tell me where I came from and how I got to Galaxitron?" Kurala urged.

"Well, I promised never to tell. . . all of us were sworn to secrecy by Shamo. He'd torture us unmercifully if any of us had revealed anything to you. I've always been loyal to Shamo . . ." Shakarr was beginning to ramble.

"Shakarr, listen carefully. Shamo is gone and you and I are the only ones left. I may well be dead in a few days after we meet with Quintron. I know he's got something unpleasant planned for me. Before I die, or before we are parted, I need to know my origins. I need to know who I am. Please tell me and help me be at peace with myself." Both Kurala and Shakarr were overcome with emotion. "Please Shakarr, please tell me!"

"All right, I guess it's O.K. You promise you won't be mad at me? I was just following orders, you know," Shakarr said.

"I won't be upset, unless you *don't* tell me," Kurala replied firmly.

"Well, we set up a trap in the grids to capture you, that's cause Shamo needed a bride and didn't want to marry a spider lady. You've heard about what they can do to you, haven't you?" he explained.

"Yes, of course, I have; but Shakarr, where did I come from?" Kurala interrupted impatiently.

"Why you are an Angel from the Celestial Realms, didn't you know that?" Shakarr said.

"Me, an Angel, are you sure?" Shakarr vigorously nodded his head up and down. "How could I possibly be an Angel? Where are my wings?" she asked incredulously.

"When you first arrived at Galaxitron you had wings. They were sort of tattered and torn from getting stuck in our trap – all covered with sticky dust too, as I remember. Well, as part of our process of restructuring you so you could marry Shamo, we cut off what was left of your wings. You're not mad at me are you? They weren't in very good shape and probably wouldn't work any more, even if you still had them," he stammered nervously.

Kurala was in absolute shock. "Me of all people, an Angel! Then how come I was so cruel and ruthless?" she asked.

"That was probably because of our restructuring at the time you lost your wings. You sort of looked like you were dying while we were doing a lot of work rearranging your inner circuitry so you could live in our energy field," he explained.

"So that's where that terrible destructive urge in me came from," Kurala realized. She wondered to herself if falling in love with AAla-dar had served to heal much of her inner circuitry, remembering that she had begun to change tremendously after their first meeting on Deneb.

Kurala knew that she now needed to be alone. There was much for her to think about. Thanking Shakarr, she quietly led him out the door.

Standing before her mirror, she looked at herself like never before. This was the face of an Angel staring back at her? How could that be? Yet, she knew that Shakarr had spoken the truth; he would have no reason to lie to her. Dressed in a tight purple silk jumpsuit, she certainly didn't dress like Angels were supposed to dress. If only she could remember back before she had been captured by the spider people. Probably the restructurization process had erased her memories.

Looking into her own eyes and noting the depth of pain which they expressed, Kurala felt like she was seeing herself for the first time. "How could they allow an Angel to get into so much trouble down here?" she wondered. "Why didn't my people come and rescue me?" This made Kurala feel truly abandoned and dispairingly lonely for the first time. The woman's eyes staring back at her were filled with compassionate sorrow and then reassurance that, somehow, everything would be all right in the end. How could her eyes in the mirror make her feel better? Wasn't she seeing the same reflection of what she was? How come the face in the mirror was full of loving reassurance and she wasn't? This was getting too confusing!

Kurala noticed that the energy levels on her ship were getting pretty strange. It felt like they were being bounced between vacuum fields. There was an echoing whooo-whooo-whuuu sound as their warship passed through a system of energy baffles. They must be traveling through Zeta Reticulum's magnetic field.

It was time for her to change into one of her prettiest garments, maybe the long copper colored dress which wrapped around her body in sinuous spirals. She'd been saving this one for a special occasion and today definitely qualified.

Returning to the command deck, Kurala gazed out the windows at a vista of unrelenting greyness. Dust storms swirled by filling the skies with scattered ashes and debris. They flew past pockmarked fragments of moons which looked like monuments of devastation. Once upon a time, there must have been one huge war here! They experienced more sudden jolts of whooo-whooo-whuuu as they passed through more baffles.

All the planets they flew by were various shades of grey, yet Kurala knew that somewhere was one which had red on it. Quintron wouldn't make a mistake like that. He knew his way around the universe better than almost anyone. He'd certainly picked a lovely place for their meeting, lots of rotten atmosphere.

Off in the distance near the far horizon, Kurala could make out a blinking red light, possibly a satellite or transmitter station. Setting course towards the beacon, focused on holding its beam steadily in front of them through the shifting grey clouds of particulate matter, she did not notice that they were now being followed by several small, grey, metallic ships.

Arriving at the beacon which was a small transmitter station suspended in space, placed there specially for her arrival by Quintron, Kurala glanced around her for the red planet they were seeking. And there it was, off to the left and downwards, a planet of ominous red and grey swirls.

Almost certain that she would meet her doom on this unnamed planet, Kurala considered having her ship drop her off at the space station and make a run to safety. But there were few crew left on the ship; besides Shakarr wouldn't be able to survive for long without her. Suddenly, there was a large WHOOSH and everyone aboard was thrown onto the floor. Picking herself up with dignity, Kurala realized that they had left the magnetic field zone and entered the gravitational pull of the red planet.

As the Galaxitron crew made their approach, Kurala made the final preparations for her meeting with Commander Quintron.

Chapter Twenty Seven:
THE NET

The black warship with a purple orchid landed gracefully at the space station on the unnamed planet. Kurala waited nervously aboard her ship waiting for some sign of welcome. No one appeared. They tried communicating with the tower, and although there were blinking lights emanating from it, no one responded. Shakarr was beside himself with fear.

"Let's get out of here, Kurala, plee-ase!" he begged shamelessly.

"No, we will wait for Quintron. He probably just hasn't arrived yet and should be here anytime. I wish that he had picked a planet with better energy though. This must be his stupid idea of a bad joke, trying to scare us," she replied.

"Well, it worked! I'm definitely scared! So let's get out of here!" Shakarr rattled with terror.

Kurala admitted to herself that she was also afraid and Shakarr wasn't making things easier by his whimpering. Maybe it *would* be smarter if they left this place, the quicker the better.

"O.K. Shakarr, let's get ready to take off; we've had enough of this grim planet."

Kurala moved to the bridge as they prepared to ascend. As they became airborne, a curious thing happened. Everytime their ship reached a certain altitude of ascent, it was as if a ceiling had been placed above them. They could only go up so far. Each time they hit an invisible barrier which bounced them back downwards.

With mounting frustration, Kurala tried to remove the energy shield by shooting it with lasers and photon beams. The barrier remained in position. She even considered throwing her ship into hyperspace, but that would be suicide for sure. Most star systems were cluttered with too many planetary bodies to propel your way through in hyperspace. All they had to do was to hit one of those deformed moon fragments and they would be thrown into another dimension by the heightened impact created by hyperspace thrust.

"Great welcome, Quintron!" Kurala muttered angrily as she rammed into the barrier again. She attempted to slide under and around the energy shield, but met with no success. Finally giving up, the warship from Galaxitron landed awkwardly on the runway.

Instantly it was surrounded by a multitude of small, grey craft which rained down from the sky relentlessly. Curious looking beings began to emerge from the space station and the crafts, walking rapidly towards her ship. Several of them held photon detonators, ready to throw.

"Come out of your ship now, alien intruders," announced a metallic voice.

"Come-out-immediately-or-we-will-vaporize-you."

"Well, I guess that I have no choice but to disembark," said Kurala. Of all the possible traps that she had considered, this was something she had never thought of. She pondered briefly whether Quintron had been captured by these grey beings too, but they hadn't seen any signs of his ship. Besides he wouldn't be traveling alone, he'd bring along at least a squadron with him.

Kurala gave her crew strict orders to remain on board and to defend the ship for as long as they were able. It was her plan to try to buy Shakarr and her crew their freedom if she could. Giving the sobbing Shakarr a final embrace, Kurala stepped out of her hatch with dignity and courage, doing her best to remember that she was not only the Queen of Galaxitron, but an Angel from the Celestial Realms where these sort of terrifying events must be regarded as mere illusions.

She was instantly encircled by hordes of weird looking beings. Their bodies, of a semi-transparent greyish white, were short and skinny making her tower over them. Kurala did her best to emanate detached authority while she stared at them with repressed revulsion. One of the worst things about them were their oversized, elongated heads containing large black eyes which stared at her penetratingly. All she could see within the multitudes of black eyes focused upon her, were mirrored reflections upon mirrored reflections of herself. It was truly bizarre!

"What are you doing on our planet?
What are you doing on our planet?
What-are-you-doing-on-our-planet?

Why did you come to Reticulum?
Why did you come to Reticulum?
Why-did-you-come-to-Reticulum?

How dare you enter where you have not been invited!
How dare you enter where you have not been invited!
How-dare-you-enter-where-you-have-not-been-invited!"

The weird beings reproached her in a din of metallic echoings. They seemed to speak several stepped down forms of language which made them confusing to listen to.

"Can you please answer me on just one vibrational level? It's very hard to communicate with you otherwise." Kurala spoke in a tone of friendly arrogance, hoping it would give the desired impression of strength. "I came to this planet because I was invited here by Commander Quintron of the UNA Command who surely must be a friend of yours. Is he here yet?"

"We-have-never-heard-of-anyone-named-Commander-Quintron,-never,-never! Therefore,-you-must-be-lying-to-us,-so-we-will-take-you-prisoner," they replied impassively.

Although not thrilled with the course this conversation was taking, Kurala was somewhat relieved that, at least, they were speaking through only one step down station.

"Look, I have the message which I received from him inside my ship. He must have given me the wrong directions. We're terribly sorry to have troubled you. Why don't you just let us depart and we won't ever bother you again!" Kurala said sweetly.

"No,- we- would- rather- use- you- for- our- experiments. We- do- lots- of- experiments- and- abductions,- very- interesting- work. Maybe- you- would- like- us- to- impregnate- you- with- a- baby ?"

Several beings stepped forward and began to fondle the fabric of her dress. This was more than Kurala could handle. Something inside of her just snapped. Pulling out her laser weapon, she killed as many of the nasty Reticulums as she could before Kurala herself, collapsed, knocked out by a stunner.

RETURN FROM THE ABYSS

Passing through
the raging storms
of deepest night,
all is in darkness.
Hope evaporates;
despair rules now
in the realms of Death.

In the spiral vortex
of the blackest hole,
the endless tunnel
leads nowhere.
Confusion abounds,
nowhere to rest,
nothing to hold onto.

While I die and die
endlessly,
ever letting go
of everything
I once held dear.
I wonder how
I created this?

Are all we see outside
true mirrors of our soul?
Cannot it be
that the mirrors we see
sometimes
are distorted
in order to test
our sureness of Purpose
and clarity of vision?

As we pass
through this stage
of our initiation –
losing everything
and everyone,
drowning in despair,
we crash and burn.

Another black hole
has been entered
and passed through
like a succession
of merciless hells.
We are smashed
and reforged,
smashed and reforged.

Yet, something remains
when finally we emerge.
Something survives,
lessons are learned.
The planetary body
is made lighter from that
which we have transmuted.

Opening our eyes
we gaze upon the ebbing embers
of tempests past,
wondering at our survival,
in awe that Light remains
and like a wizened child
we rise and begin anew.

Chapter Twenty Eight:
THE VISITOR

The Angel stood before the assembled Council of Light of Betelguese in her fullest radiance. She emanated a pristine purity untainted by experience within this dimensional universe of duality. To describe her as merely beautiful would not do her justice for she was far more than that. She was an exquisite creature of graceful Golden Light. We shall simply note that wherever she appeared, a most delicate music could be heard – heavenly choirs softly singing anthems of love.

Her decision to journey here had not been an easy one for it is rare that Angels who haven't incarnated choose to step down their energies sufficiently to descend into the limitations of form. But that she had chosen to do out of her bounteous love. For countless years she had watched the travails of her sister from afar, sadly weeping by the light of the stars. Finally, she could bear it no longer; her help was desperately needed.

Even in the Celestial Realms, she had been strongly advised against this form of action, but she had pleaded mightily to be an instrument of Divine Intervention until it was finally agreed upon that she could go, *only* to the Council of Light, they had warned. Anything other than that would be too dangerous. Even she could get ensnared in the traps of illusion. If anything tainted her impeccability on her journey she would get stuck on the wheel of rebirth and have no choice, but to descend into matter for a full cycle of incarnations. Thus here she was, standing before the Council, asking for their advice on how she could serve her beloved sister who had suffered for so long.

"I am Luminara. I come from the Celestial Realms, traveling here in order to aid my sister whom you know as Kurala," she stated simply.

After the Council had heard her story, they sent a messenger to summon Commander AAla-dar to the Council Chambers as soon as he could be located, for it was known that he had countless experiences with the one known as Kurala.

While they were waiting for AAla-dar to arrive, the Council collectively tuned into Kurala's whereabouts and saw the events which were transpiring on Zeta Reticulum. Luminara could not watch all that she saw. Her heart welled up with sadness; perhaps she had come too late. Although she knew well that the Higher Purpose was manifest within everything, she could not understand how Kurala's tragic experiences were serving anyone or anything. What a strange and incomprehensible world this was, the world of duality and form!

At last a weary AAla-dar strode into the Council Chambers looking much perplexed. When he saw Luminara standing there with such innocence and purity he could not help but fall to his knees in awe and respect. Why had a disincarnate Angel in the purity of her Presence come to the Council? Never before had he been so honored to meet one.

AAla-dar was duly introduced to Luminara who already knew him well. She had long been aware of the love which he and Kurala shared and of the many miraculous changes it had wrought in her beloved sister.

"Commander AAla-dar, I am the sister of Kurala who is also of the Angelic Realms. She was captured long ago by the Shamo of Galaxitron and made the bride of the king of the spider people." Luminara watched him with a smile as the shock of discovering that his dear Kurala was an Angel set in. "I want to extend my gratitude to you for serving her so greatly and for the depth of your love towards her. You have helped heal her far more than I have been able to thus far. But now she is in grave danger. That is why I have come and the help of all of us is needed more than ever before."

Kurala's present situation in Zeta Reticulum was hereby described to AAla-dar by one of the members of the Council.

Filled with sorrow, AAla-dar spoke gravely, "I know those beings on Reticulum well. Their exploits have always filled me with loathing. I warned her that Commander Quintron could not be trusted. Do you want me to go there and rescue her?" He looked directly at Luminara. "You know that I love her as I have loved no other."

"No, that will not be necessary, because she is already being taken elsewhere," said Uriel-la firmly.

Luminara spoke with thoughtful simplicity, fully understanding the import of her words. "There is one place where I must journey and that is to the very heart of darkness. AAla-dar, could you take me to see the OMNI?" she asked. "They are the ones who have the power to set Kurala free."

The entire Council sat in stunned silence. Not one of them had ever made a journey to the realms of the Dark Lords. Surely it would be most dangerous, especially for an Angel unaccustomed to the perils of form.

"Luminara, we must dissuade you from traveling to the OMNI," spoke Uriel-la, full of compassionate understanding. "You have absolutely no idea of what you are getting into."

"That is where I must go," stated Luminara quietly.

"Then I shall be the one to take you there," answered AAla-dar with his usual courage.

"Please reconsider this; it is too dangerous. AAla-dar, speak to her, tell her what it entails. Luminara won't be able to handle the energies there," Uriel-la implored. "The negative energies will damage her drastically."

"AAla-dar, please take me to the OMNI," Luminara asked with shining innocence, looking straight into the depths of his soul.

"When shall we go, Luminara?" AAla-dar replied, ignoring the plaintive cries of the Council members.

"Right now. I am ready. Do you have a ship?" she asked.

"One of the best. Let's go!" he replied.

Taking his arm, Luminara departed the Council Chambers with AAla-dar. The Council sat numbed with shock, not daring to believe what had just transpired.

Thus it was that Luminara did descend from the starry heavens to rescue her sister Kurala from the illusions of duality. And thus it was that AAla-dar and Luminara did join together to travel to the home of the Dark Lords.

Chapter Twenty Nine:
AWAKENING

When Kurala awoke, she was no longer on the unnamed planet of Zeta Reticulum. Shortly after she had been felled by the stunner, they had taken her inside to prepare her for exploratory surgery. Suddenly, a loud clamorous shouting could be heard as Reticulums fled in various directions trying in vain to hide. The pinging and zapping of laser weapons reverberated with the hideous vacuum sound of photon beams vaporizing their victims into nothingness.

Several tall figures clad in black stealthily stalked into the medical laboratory and carried Kurala away. She was placed in isolation on an unmarked black ship and with the other occupants of the Galaxitron craft were rapidly removed from Reticulum.

Kurala had been finally captured by the Dark Lords of Orion. After they had received the message from Quintron offering her in exchange for a pardon of all the Trons of Maldon, a highly trained special unit of the OMNI had made haste to Reticulum to fetch their prize.

The Orion warship moved swiftly through the skies to its appointed destination of Rigel, home of the Dark Lords. Kurala was transferred to secret quarters under a heavy guard. Here she was thoroughly checked by physicians and healers who decreed that she would soon regain consciousness.

Zeon himself slipped into her room and observed her with heightened curiosity as she slept, marvelling at the beauty of this fallen Angel. Kurala's energy was such an unusual combination of the highest light mixed with her descent into the darkness. He had never encountered anyone quite like her. Zeon had been secretly watching her for years now and she was even more fascinating than he had imagined. Zeon was much amused to discover how excited he was by her presence. Vowing to protect Kurala from the other two members of the Triad, he placed some of his personal guards outside her door so that she would not be disturbed.

Shortly after Kurala began to regain consciousness, one of her attendants sent a secret summons to Zeon who rushed to her side. Opening her eyes for the first time, Kurala discovered an extremely magnetic, dark haired man standing before her, regarding her intently.

"How are you feeling, my dear?" he asked.

Kurala's eyes widened in panic. "Who are you?. . . Where am I?. . . What happened to those horrible aliens from Reticulum?" she asked, feeling severely disoriented.

"Now, now, calm down, you have nothing to fear," he said softly. "We have rescued you."

"Who are you and where am I?" she repeated weakly.

Zeon decided that it would be more fun to tell her the truth. "My name is Zeon and I am your friend. You have been rescued by the OMNI and you are on the great star system of Rigel."

"The OMNI! You are one of the OMNI!" Kurala tried to get up, but fell back limply. Her physical strength had not yet returned. It always took quite a while after getting blasted with a stunner. She closed her eyes for a few moments, then looked at Zeon carefully. He didn't look horribly evil, but then often appearances could be deceiving.

"Maybe I should leave now so you can get some more rest," Zeon said solicitously.

"No, please stay a little longer. I don't understand what has happened. Could you explain it to me again?" she asked.

"Well, it's really rather simple, Kurala. We heard that you were in trouble on Zeta Reticulum so you were rescued and brought here," Zeon answered, his voice drenched with sincerity.

"And how do you happen to know my name?" she asked.

"My dear, I have been observing your wild adventures for many years. You have been making war against us, haven't you or did I get that wrong?" he asked kindly. Zeon's voice had assumed a paternal tone. He was beginning to talk to her as if she was a naughty child.

"Yes, I have been," she answered, much confused by his friendliness. "But if I am your enemy, why are you being so nice to me?"

"Because I choose to be. I have found you quite amusing, actually. Rarely does anyone dare to declare war against us, but you did. That either takes great innocence or tremendous courage. In your case, possibly a combination of both. But I must admit, that this war has become far more serious than I ever expected it to be. All of us have suffered huge losses because of you," Zeon explained evenly.

"So now that I am your prisoner, what do you plan to do with me?" Kurala asked, too tired to care. After the Reticulums, even the Dark Lords couldn't be that bad.

"I haven't said that you are our prisoner. I told you that we rescued you. Aren't you grateful that we took you away from there? The Reticulums were in the process of preparing you for surgery." Zeon was a master of manipulation, Kurala could see that clearly.

"I am most grateful for your intervention. Thank you, Zeon. But I'm not really free to leave Rigel, am I?" she asked, managing a small smile.

"Not for the time being. It's important that you rest for a while, isn't it? You're too weak to go make war against us right now, anyway," he said with a laugh.

Kurala had to agree on that score. "What happened to the crew of my ship?" she asked with concern.

"They are here enjoying our hospitality as our *guests*. Of course, one of your spiders, the old one named Shakarr, is pretty much falling apart." Zeon found Shakarr's terror to be extremely funny.

"Zeon, is there any way you could do me a favor and send Shakarr a message letting him know that I'm alright?" she asked.

"For you, of course my dear." He called for one of the attendants to enter and had Kurala write a short note to Shakarr, which he immediately dispatched with one of his guards. "Anything else I can do for you? Would you like some Vega wafers, as I remember you're quite fond of them?" said Zeon with a broad smile, thoroughly enjoying himself.

"Maybe later, Zeon. You seem to know almost everything about me. Can't you tell me what you're going to do to me? Am I going to be killed or tortured or what?" she said.

"Dear Kurala, you've had more than enough to think about for today. You don't need anything else to worry about. Why don't you have a little rest? Maybe I'll visit you later tonight." Zeon bent forward, kissed her softly on the forehead and departed.

Totally confused as to the reality of her situation, Kurala closed her eyes and returned to sleep.

Δ   Δ   Δ

Chapter Thirty:
DOUBLE-CROSS

Thoroughly exhausted, Kurala slept through the night, heedless of Zeon's silent nocturnal visit. For several hours he sat in a chair by her bedside watching her sleep, wondering at the content of her dreams. She stirred something deep within him, although he could not describe what it was. Possibly it had something to do with the fact that she was an Angel who had not chosen to descend into matter, but had fallen into form quite against her will. Or maybe it was because he had never before encountered a woman of such strength and depth. Whatever it was, he loved observing her.

The other two members of the OMNI had heard of Kurala's capture and were anxious to get their revenge with her. He was going to have to do something about them so they didn't harm her. Not yet, anyway, they would have to wait until he was finished with her. Zeon had procured false medical reports which greatly exaggerated her condition, saying that she would not be regaining consciousness for weeks. That should buy him some time, he reasoned. And he hadn't really decided what to do with her, after all.

Of course, she should be punished, for she had made war against the OMNI and should be used as an example for others not to cross them. But there was something about her that penetrated right to the depths of that small circle of white embedded within his aura, which none of the Dark Lords knew that he possessed. Zeon felt that he was responsible for her well being and protection, although he didn't yet know why that was so important. Kurala belonged to him and to him alone, and no one else would tamper with her while he was in charge.

Zeon had a plan which should serve to draw the focus away from Kurala. He had sent a message to Commander Quintron praising him for his actions and asking him to meet with the OMNI on Rigel to discuss the terms of their treaty with Maldon. Quintron had answered immediately and would be arriving on Rigel soon. It would be easy to double-cross a double-crosser!

While he was awaiting Quintron's arrival, Zeon continued his daily visits with Kurala. He felt that he was slowly gaining her confidence. Kurala was recovering rapidly and was beginning to sit up in bed and eat Vega wafers. Once he had even had old Shakarr smuggled into her room in a basket of bed linens so they could have a short visit. That seemed to endear him further with Kurala, for she had been deeply touched by Zeon's act of compassion.

"Zeon, there is one thing I truly don't understand," Kurala asked one day. "How can you be such a kind person if you are the head of the OMNI? I know that you're not this way all the time. I've heard so many stories about your terrible deeds and you're the ones who put those awful implants into Shamo. It just doesn't make any sense."

And then, in spite of himself, Zeon told her what he had never shared with anyone. He explained about his circle of white.

"And it is decreed from On High that one of the OMNI shall always carry this sphere of white, unbeknownst to any of the others?" she asked with rising fascination.

Zeon nodded affirmatively. "Yes, and it's quite a responsibility."

"Since this universe is anchored under a template of duality, does this also mean that one of the members of the Council of Light also carries within him a circle of dark?" she asked.

Kurala was a highly intelligent woman. She had just guessed what few had ever known. "Yes, somewhere within the Council of Light there is someone who has a circle of darkness. At the present moment it is carried by a woman. I don't know her name, but I constantly feel her presence. It's as if we are somehow linked together; possibly she is my female counterpart or twin flame," Zeon replied.

"And no one else on either Council knows of the existence of this?" Kurala said with mounting interest.

"No one, except her and me and now you. Of course, on other realms within the zone of overlap, there is a being who knows, for he holds the key to the template of duality," he said.

"And what is the name of the one who holds the key?" she asked.

"He is called Metatron. He's the overseer of the All-Seeing Eye of AN and holds the responsibility for the entire zone of overlap. Being the bearers of these spheres of dark and light gives me and the woman in the Council of Light direct access into both the zone of overlap and the All-Seeing Eye. But of course, we are not allowed to misuse our power or overstep the boundaries of our chosen areas of service. We must play out our roles in duality as if they were real and truly mattered. Yet, all the while, we must remember, first and foremost, that we are only playing out parts in a grand, cosmic play."

Zeon continued, "Kurala, it is important that you

never reveal this to anyone. For some reason, I know it is appropriate that I share this knowledge with you. I have never spoken of it to anyone before, but I have received direct guidance that you were to be told. If you should ever attempt to divulge this secret, I would have to prevent you rather forcefully." Zeon's threat was said with such tenderness that Kurala could only agree with him on its appropriateness.

"Zeon, don't worry, I will keep your trust. I promise not to reveal your secret," she replied.

There was a sudden knock on the door. Zeon held a hushed conversation with one of the guards. "I must go now, my dear. There is a visitor whom I must attend to, but I will return later." Again he kissed her tenderly upon the forehead which he did every time he departed.

Δ

Commander Quintron, newly arrived, was being presented to the Triad of the OMNI. He was full of his usual swagger, confidant of impending victory. Maybe he would finally gain some respect for bringing to an end this terrible intergalactic war.

"Well, I'm glad to finally meet you. I've heard a lot about you; you guys are pretty famous, you know," Quintron drawled, while carefully checking out the infamous Triad.

Two of them looked pretty heavy. The short, fat one obviously had a terrible temper and was ready to erupt any second. Dangerous, but predictable. The tall thin one was more devious – cold and calculating for sure. You wouldn't want to turn your back on that one. But it was the middle one that he had to watch out for. Quintron could tell that the middle one held the real power around here. He was awfully handsome for a Dark Lord, sort of inscrutable actually. "I'll have to be real careful around him," Quintron thought to himself.

"Pleased to meet you, Commander Quintron. I am Zeon and this is Triax and Narcron," the middle one explained politely. "How was your journey?"

"Fine, it went real easy. Thanks for the escort. Did you capture Kurala?" Quintron asked.

"Yeah, but she was half dead when our people got there," Narcron whispered menacingly, subtly implying that it was all Quintron's fault.

"Why did you send her to Reticulum? We wanted her in better shape, not half dead. We've got lots of plans for her," Triax added angrily.

"What do you mean half dead? Is Kurala going to be all-right?" Quintron asked with a sense of rising concern. He had been so furious at Kurala over Kowtron's death that he hadn't really allowed himself to think about what the Dark Lords might do to her.

"She should recover in a few more weeks. The Reticulums had taken her prisoner and were about to do their gruesome surgery on her," Narcron said in a whispery whine of accusation.

"We wanted her alive, in good condition," Triax repeated stubbornly.

"Well, what are you going to do with her, now that she's here?" Quintron asked, wondering why suddenly he cared so much about Kurala.

Triax rubbed his hands together with glee. "Oh, we'll probably begin with some slow torture, maybe the erotic kind. Then she'll be filled with implants so we can get some use out of her. After the implants are activated, we'll send her back to the war, this time working for us. Eventually, of course, she'll be murdered, unless we can think of something more exciting to do."

Narcron just smiled in silent agreement with Triax.

Quintron was no fool. Squinting, he watched Zeon carefully out of the corner of his eyes to see what his response was to all this. Zeon kept his perceptions tightly veiled. That guy's energy was really hard to read. Maybe if he could be alone with him, they might talk frankly, but who knows? That Zeon was a real, cool professional, not many like him around. No wonder that he'd been made head of the OMNI!

"Well, have you drawn up a treaty for us?" Quintron changed the subject abruptly. He didn't want to think about Kurala anymore or he might start feeling guilty.

"No, we haven't," said Zeon with quiet authority. "Instead we've decided that you're just as guilty as Kurala. She wouldn't have ever gotten her war started if you hadn't joined forces and supplied her with ships and arms."

Quintron was shocked. "Hey, wait a minute man. A deal's a deal. You promised our freedom if we delivered Kurala to you. The lady's here and we demand what's coming to us!" he shouted angrily.

"You are definitely going to receive what's coming to you," Zeon replied calmly. "You are now our prisoner. We have already taken into custody the squadrons which you brought here with you. For such a notorious outlaw, you're pretty naive and trusting, aren't you? I thought you'd be a lot smarter. Don't you believe the nasty stories you hear about us?" Zeon was becoming amused by the stunned look on Quintron's face.

"Hey, is this a joke or what? Come on you guys, this ain't funny! You're trying to double-cross me. I demand that you set me free!" Quintron's face was flushed with fury.

Triax pointed his chubby finger at Quintron who collapsed on the floor twitching in stupefying pain. Triax opened his mouth in a snarly grin. "That shut him up! Stupid cowboy, who does he think he is, anyway?"

"O.K. Triax, that is enough!" Zeon ordered.

Remaining on the floor, his body drenched in sweat, Quintron wiped away his tears. "Oh, man, you've got a powerful finger. Well, you made your point; I'm impressed. Now are you going to honor your promise and let us go?"

"Take him to a cell," Zeon called impassively to the guards and turned away with disinterest.

Yelling and brawling with anger, Commander Quintron was led away.

Chapter Thirty One:
RIGEL

Aboard his starship, the considerable skills of Triple Commander AAla-dar were about to be severely tested. The journey from Betelgeuse to Rigel was not vast as distances in space are measured, but it was a difficult one for it entailed bridging two extremely different energy patternings. This could be compared to flying from fire into ice; the underlying vibrational currents were that dissimilar.

This drastic shift in energy affected the composition of the star waves themselves whose density matrices measured on the opposite ends of the scale within the two zones of Orion. In order to leave one zone and enter the next, a recalibration of phasar thrust meters must be undertaken quickly and thoroughly. If this wasn't done immediately upon leaving the zone of light, one would run aground in the thicker density patterning of the zone of dark. When reversing direction and traveling from dark to light, the recalibration would serve to slow down the ship so it would not overshoot its mark and end up in a distant galaxy.

As AAla-dar prepared for their imminent entry into the patterning of the Dark Lords, he knew that not only would he have to move his ship into hyperthrust overdrive to keep at their present speed, but he would have to invent some original maneuvers to keep their ship from being shot down by the Dark Lords. He had already activated their shields of invisibility which would serve to keep them unnoticed until they got closer to the realms of the Councils of Dark. Within a certain radius of Rigel, they would surely be noticed and attacked, for no one was allowed to enter Rigel uninvited.

Glancing over at Luminara, he saw that she was still meditating as she had for most of their voyage. A soft, yet strong Golden Light emanated from her radiant form, so serenely beautiful and innocent. AAla-dar hoped that he would be able to fulfill his promise to her and take her to the OMNI. How incredible that this exquisite being was the sister of Kurala! He found it amusing to imagine his wildly independent Kurala sitting in deep meditation with such a purity of Presence, and yet knew, that it must have once been so. "Why had Kurala fallen into such darkness?" he wondered. "What Purpose did it serve?" And what was his involvement in this drama?"

AAla-dar dared not turn his attention to the fate of Kurala, merely decreeing that she was alive and safe, possibly in Rigel. Being in the hands of the Dark Lords couldn't be worse than the treacherous inhabitants of Zeta Reticulum. He made a silent prayer that he would find Kurala and rescue her. This time he wouldn't leave her, even if it meant resigning from the Confederation.

These thoughts were abruptly broken as the ship began to bounce roughly through the flotsam of the transition zone. AAla-dar and his crew proceeded to recalibrate their instrument panels with lightning fast precision. Luminara calmly glanced over at their wild gyrations with a loving smile, paying no attention to the violent rocking of the ship which jerked about each time that it hit a density pocket. The Angel was in total trust of the impeccability of their Mission and knew that their passage to the OMNI would be unhindered.

Star Commander AAla-dar wished that he shared her certainty. He was having difficulty keeping their ship stable as it was being bombarded with erratic frequency bursts. If it got too wildly out of control, the hyperthrust mechanism would have little effect in propelling them forward. Once his crew got the gyros recalibrated, they would be able to deploy the super-stabilizers. Working silently with concentrated focus, they knew that a few moments delay could mean disaster.

Finally the hyperthrust overdrive kicked on while spurts of electric blue flames were emitted at the rear of his starship. They forged ahead in spurts like moving through sticky mud until they were finally freed from the goo. The density switchover had been successfully completed. AAla-dar gave his crew a grateful look of silent approval. Luminara smiled at them all as if they were off on a picnic, just having a quiet peaceful day. That she was so unruffled, made AAla-dar laugh out loud which helped to dissolve the accumulated tension. Soon everyone was laughing with delight, although none of them could have told you why.

Flying ever closer to Rigel through realms of dark-ness, always flying towards the danger of the unknown, they continued on through layers of night. Before departing Betelgeuse, AAla-dar had carefully briefed his crew who had all volunteered for this journey. The perils of the mission had been spoken of openly and no one was encouraged to come. Yet out of love for their Commander, out of deep loyalty and respect, the finest in his command had chosen to accompany him on this fateful journey.

Suddenly the dark sky filled with small black war-ships flying in formation of a V. The air was illuminated with dramatic displays in brilliant fluorescent colors of the latest laser technology. Quickly glancing behind him, AAla-dar noted that another squadron had them cut off at the rear.

"Luminara, we are surrounded by Orion warships. It appears as if we have flown right into a huge trap. We don't have many options, if any, but I'll give it everything I've got," he reported with weary resignation, for truly AAla-dar couldn't think of anything to do except try to blast an opening through the approaching formation which looked pretty invincible.

"I have a suggestion, AAla-dar," Luminara said quietly. "Before you do anything, could you please send a message to the head of the OMNI, I believe his name is Zeon, telling him that we are coming to meet with him and requesting full rights of passage. An escort service to Rigel would be nice, too. Make sure you tell him that this is an Alpha Code Frequency Link Up, by Supreme Command of the Council of the Elohim." She smiled at him brightly. "Don't worry AAla-dar, he will let us through with no problem."

And sure enough, that was exactly what happened. As soon as the message was sent, the approaching squadron opened up its tight formation and made way for them to pass right through the middle of the V. Two warships came alongside and signalled for them to follow. Safe passage to Rigel was given. Luminara laughed with delight; she was thoroughly enjoying her adventure into form. AAla-dar had never seen anything like it; he'd have to remember to say that he was from the Council of the Elohim if he ever came this way again.

The Star System of Rigel itself was quite impressive. Tall, black volcanic peaks punctuated the horizon, half hidden by reddish mists of smoke and blowing volcanic ash, giving everything an aura of deep, impenetrable mystery and power. Random rivers of molten lava glowed like ribbons of light – vast clouds of steam rising where fire flowed into water. And there were the famous winds of Rigel, peaceful for much of the time like sleeping giants. Then without warning, the winds would rise and blow, relentlessly scouring the landscape until all activities came to a halt and everything submitted itself to a more powerful force. Rigel was an unusual combination of raw primordial energy mixed with the most highly developed technology available.

As the spaceport came into view, they prepared to land, following the descent of their two escort ships with ease. It was decided that only AAla-dar and Luminara would disembark. This was often the rule, followed not only for safety – in case the crew needed to make a fast getaway, but often a practical necessity as well, since there was such a variation in substance and appearance among lifestreams.

A small black bullet craft approached their ship and patiently waited for our two passengers to descend. Seated in the craft, AAla-dar and Luminara were whisked off to the sacred city of Ra-Matah, capitol of Rigel and home of the Council of the Dark Lords.

Chapter Thirty Two:
RA-MATAH

Upon entering the ancient walled city of Ra-Matah, AAla-dar was struck by its aura of mystery. Myriad crooked, winding narrow streets like a casbah branched out from broad straight avenues which were the central thoroughfares. Both on ground and in the air, bullet cars zoomed by in great profusion. But as they passed by the smaller, twisting roads he could see ancient looking people walking about clad in long black robes immersed in the activities of everyday life. These pathways must be reserved for pedestrians, he thought. There was something about these small avenues which fascinated AAla-dar. Each vignette that he saw there as they passed by was timeless, portraying myriad scenes of the pathos of life.

At the far end of the city, high upon a hill was the palace of Ra-Matah. It could best be described as black, shiny, elegant, opulent and high tech. Our two travelers were quietly welcomed by Zeon's private security guards and hurriedly taken to a secret meeting room for an audience with the head of the Dark Lords himself.

Gazing about him, AAla-dar observed the many fascinating details of the room which was decorated in an interesting combination of matte black metal and deep purple velvet. Colored lights were recessed into the wall behind fixtures of delicate silver tracery in the shapes of magical symbols. There was a variety of elegant velvet couches and chairs to sit upon. On the wall was a highly complex, computerized control panel which sent forth operatic music. AAla-dar paced the room carefully, noting its lack of windows and that everything within it was carefully controlled.

A hidden door opened soundlessly and Zeon suddenly made his entrance. He and AAla-dar stared at each other in silence, sizing the other carefully and finding their counterpart both capable and honorable. Using the intergalactic salute, they respectfully introduced themselves.

At this point Luminara looked up from her meditations and smiled lovingly at Zeon. "Well hello Zeon, I've been looking forward to meeting you," she said while taking his hand warmly. "Let me introduce myself properly." She stood up and shared her mudra with great reverence. "I AM LUMINARA and I come from the Elohim." Gesturing for Zeon and AAla-dar to sit down, Luminara returned to her chair.

"Zeon we have come here because of my sister Kurala," began Luminara. "First I'd like to know where she is." Her eyes pierced into Zeon with quiet authority.

"She is here with us in Ra-Matah, actually within this very palace," Zeon replied evenly. Then while he noted the shooting sparks within AAla-dar's eyes at the mention of Kurala, he continued. "And she is doing well. She has fully recovered from being stunned on Reticulum." Turning to AAla-dar, he said pointedly, "Kurala is in *my* custody and is enjoying my full protection." Zeon was surprised to discover within himself feelings of jealousy over Kurala. He really wanted to keep her all to himself.

"Will you bring Kurala here to meet with us?" AAla-dar asked. He was suddenly getting the feeling that

Zeon might be in love with Kurala and that it might not be so easy to get her released.

"That doesn't feel appropriate at the present moment. It would merely serve to upset Kurala and make her confused. Please note that I haven't indicated that Kurala is free to leave from my custody," Zeon said. Then smiling charmingly at Luminara, he said, "But if her lovely sister wants a glimpse of her while she is sleeping, simply to set her heart at ease, I could arrange that."

"No, that won't be necessary," said Luminara, surprising everyone. "I don't need to see her on the physical. And we certainly haven't come to forcibly rescue her from your grasp, so you needn't worry yourself about her escaping," she reassured Zeon who was becoming somewhat confused.

"Well, what would you like to do then?" he asked.

"I need to spend some time alone with you Zeon," she replied calmly. "I am called to journey where none have gone before. I wish to travel to the Source *beyond* the OMNI, to that which lies hidden and you are my doorway. This door could be perceived as a small circle of white. Do you understand now?" Luminara smiled sweetly at Zeon.

The leader of the OMNI sat in shocked silence. Never could he have anticipated this request. What did it truly signify? Somewhere within him, he knew that he could not deny Luminara's request, no matter what the consequences would be. And there was no question that there would be serious consequences set into motion by this unprecedented action.

Luminara gazed deeply into Zeon's eyes while emanating all-encompassing love. It was as if she had already locked herself into that sphere of white within him. He could not push her out nor deny her request.

"Alright, you shall have your wish," Zeon replied

with effort, barely managing to pull his eyes away from hers. He was overwhelmed with a deep longing to experience new depths of love as he looked into Luminara's eyes.

Remembering the presence of the Star Commander, Zeon turned to him and said, "AAla-dar, I shall have to send you to your quarters. You will be well tended to as long as you don't try to interfere with Kurala." Zeon pushed some buttons on the control panel and whispered hushed commands. The door opened and three guards stood ready to accompany AAla-dar to his quarters.

As the Star Commander glanced at Luminara for her approval, she spoke firmly, "Go, dear one and worry not. While you are waiting in your room, communicate with Kurala through the love in your heart. She will feel it and respond. Whether I see you again or not, know that I am well and eternally protected. Remember that the Higher Purpose is always being served. Question not the small details, but serve the whole with unflinching trust and commitment." She stood and embraced AAla-dar, infusing him with Golden Light. "Thank you for your help and for your dedicated service. It shall not be forgotten."

Deeply moved, AAla-dar bowed to the Angel Luminara, possibly the most radiant Presence he had ever beheld and departed the room.

Turning to each other, Zeon and Luminara sat close together, their eyes burning through layers upon layers returning to purest Essence. The Angel was about to journey where no one had ever gone before. Zeon knew that he must let her pass through the central core of his being.

Focusing with her totality upon the sphere of white hidden deep within Zeon, Luminara merged herself into it and thus stepped through the doorway.

ΔΔΔ

Chapter Thirty Three:
THE COUNCIL OF DARK

Early in the morning during the time of heightened primal darkness which always heralds a new dawn, messengers were sent forth summoning the entire Council of Dark to an important emergency session. Some of the prisoners and guests of the OMNI were roused from their rooms as well and brought into the Council Chambers. Even Kurala came for she could no longer be hidden under the protection of Zeon. His invincibility had been fatefully compromised.

Members of the Council arrived in an uproar of unfounded rumors and confusion. Not knowing what to expect, Kurala entered the chambers and was quickly given a front row seat in the rectangular shaped Council. Shortly thereafter, Commander Quintron arrived with his usual brash confidence clad in cowboy boots and sunglasses, certain that he was finally going to receive his deserved reprieve. Kurala looked at him in disbelief for she had certainly not expected to encounter Quintron on Rigel.

"Quintron, what are you doing here?" she whispered as he passed by.

"Hey, baby, I'm glad to see that you're here," Quintron said, much relieved that she was still alive. He noticed that she was even more fetching than the last time he had seen her. "Look Kurala, I'm sorry about my little trick at Reticulum. I was pretty pissed off about Kowtron. I hope you don't have any hard feelings. Uh, do you forgive me?" Quintron was pushed along by the Dark Lords guarding him before Kurala had time to answer. They seated him 90' away on the side to her right where they could still maintain eye contact.

She couldn't believe that Quintron was a prisoner here. And did he really expect her to forgive him?, she thought with indignation. But then again, why not? What really mattered anymore, now that they were all the prisoners of the Dark Lords? Maybe this brutal and tedious war would finally end and who knows, perhaps somehow she and Quintron would manage to survive.

"Kurala!" Turning around in her seat, Kurala looked straight at AAla-dar! Immediately, her eyes filled with tears. Reaching up to him with love, Kurala tenderly touched his face. "Oh AAla-dar, you're here too!"

Overcome with emotion, AAla-dar could not speak. Taking her hand he pressed her fingers to his lips. Neither of them could pull their eyes away from the other until one of the Dark Lords roughly shoved AAla-dar aside and indicated his seat. Now AAla-dar, Kurala and Quintron all were sitting in the front row of the Council, each one on a different side, forming a triangle.

Watching with interest, Quintron saw the obvious love and familiarity between Kurala and AAla-dar. "So that's who she went to visit on Mebsuta," he thought. Grudgingly he had to admit that AAla-dar wasn't such a bad choice for Kurala. But why was AAla-dar here on Rigel? Had he come to rescue Kurala? If so, he was a lot crazier than he thought.

While this silent drama between the three was being enacted, there was another observer carefully noting each nuance and relationship among the newcomers to the Council. Zeon sat quietly in his deep purple velvet chair located directly across from Kurala. His fascination with her was further heightened by the crosscurrents flowing through the Council.

Suddenly Kurala could feel a gaze boring into her and looked up to discover Zeon's eyes staring at her intently from across the room. She noticed immediately that Zeon's energy was vastly different than before; something very powerful had happened to him. Her eyes implored him to reassure her that everything was going to be all right. But this Zeon could not do, for much was uncertain.

And please be certain to note that AAla-dar and Quintron, transfixed by Kurala's presence, were now made well aware of her close connection with Zeon. The rectangular Council Chamber had Zeon sitting in the front row, Quintron on the side to his left, Kurala directly across from Zeon and AAla-dar on the side to his right. They were now in their appointed positions.

During all this time, the Council was not in a state of static calm. Rather the chambers boiled with a palpable anguish, expressing copious arguments while several small fights erupted. Triax was in his element, yelling and brawling while Narcron stealthily stalked through the aisles, spreading whispers of deceit.

Finally Zeon called the Council to order. As he stood up to get everyone's attention, Kurala noted the depth of his transformation. Zeon was streaming with radiance, becoming evermore transparent as she watched. Something profound had happened last night, she thought, wishing that she could talk to him in private.

The leader of the OMNI spoke with unusual difficulty as if forgetting how to form his words. "Last night there was a shift, possibly a breach, within the invincibility of the OMNI. We received a visitor from the Council of the Elohim who arrived with a request which I could not deny and which only I could fulfill. This visitor was the sister of the woman Kurala whom you see sitting opposite me today."

At this point, the entire Council turned to stare at Kurala, some rising to openly threaten her. Both AAladar and Quintron stood ready to defend her if necessary. Kurala herself, listened to Zeon in shock. Who was this sister of hers and where was she now?

"Sit down everyone and leave Kurala alone. If you would learn to listen, we might be able to proceed a lot quicker." Zeon was feeling impatient because he had much to do and time was running out. He could see that Narcron had moved next to Triax and was whispering intensely into his ear. Of course, they would recognize his time of weakness and be ready to make their move.

The Council returned to order, possibly because they were aware that something was terribly wrong. Zeon continued, "The intergalactic war is over. Orders have already been given for our forces to disband. Messages have been sent to the Intergalactic Confederation notifying them of our actions. As you can see, we have the leaders of the upstart UNA forces here with us as well as one of the Commanders from the Confederation. It is my recommendation that they be . . . *(ping, ping)*. . set . . . *(ping, ping, ping)*. . . free . . ." Zeon faltered here and turned around. Behind him stood Narcron and Triax. They had just shot Zeon's back full of poison laser darts. The leader of the OMNI fell to the floor lifeless, and the Council erupted in pandemonium!

"Death to the traitor!" shouted Triax and Narcron in unison.

Kurala tried to rush to Zeon's aid, but was held back by two of the Dark Lords. AAla-dar and Quintron were also quickly placed into custody and the three of them were hurriedly removed from the room. A bullet car was waiting outside and as soon as they were pushed inside, it sped away through the busy avenues of Ra-Matah.

187

Chapter Thirty Four:
A NEW LORD

There was no time to talk or even think, so quickly did they travel. AAla-dar, Kurala & Quintron huddled together in one seat while three Dark Lords sat behind them. In the front there were two more who drove through the skyways with lightning fast precision.

Kurala, still sobbing, rested her head upon AAla-dar's shoulder and held Quintron's arm for support. The scenery outside had become a blur. After some moments, they came to a stop outside of an unmarked building. Dark hooded robes were handed to them to put on. Then they were ushered inside the building which appeared to be a warehouse of some kind. Exiting by the rear doors, they found themselves on a narrow, twisting path right in the heart of Ra-Matah. Now they were led down a labyrinthean system of streets, each one becoming smaller and darker.

Finally, they came to a locked gate which was quickly opened with a sonar device by one of the Dark Lords. Entering a small courtyard, they climbed up a stairway into what appeared to be a villa. After the curtains had been pulled tight, the room was lighted. Yes, they seemed to be in a private residence. There were five Dark Lords with them, all of whom slowly dropped their hoods, revealing four men and one woman.

"Please sit down and make yourselves comfortable," one of the men whispered. "You will be safe here, at least for a while."

"Who are you and why did you bring us here?" Kurala asked.

"I am Lord Lormax. We are all members of Zeon's personal staff. He had a premonition that he might not survive this Council meeting, so we put together this escape plan. We might as well tell you that we didn't rescue you simply out of altruism. Now that Zeon is dead, our lives are in danger too. But with you in our custody, we shall have better bargaining power. We're going to return to the Council and see if we can influence things there. You'll be left alone for a while, but we've got guards outside, so don't try anything funny. Besides, this is probably the safest place for you in Ra-Matah right now. Do you understand?"

AAla-dar nodded in agreement. "Thanks for the rescue. If you hadn't come along, we'd probably all be dead by now."

The Dark Lords quickly departed leaving an awkward silence. Kurala wished that she was alone with AAla-dar, for now that the danger was past, Quintron was returning to his old, arrogant self.

"Well baby, you never told me you had a boyfriend," he began accusingly.

"Look Quintron, after all that you've put me through, I don't even want to talk to you," Kurala retorted.

AAla-dar watched them carefully, sensing the bond between them. He could see that Quintron desired Kurala, which was why she constantly infuriated him.

"Well, I don't go around killing your best friend," Quintron snarled.

"No, you just murder people's husbands," Kurala replied testily.

"Yeah, well that disgusting spider was full of Orion implants," he said.

189

"Um, excuse me," AAla-dar interjected, "before you go on any further, don't you think we could put this time to better use? Maybe we could discuss possible ways to get out of here alive?"

Somewhat ashamed that AAla-dar should see her acting so childishly, Kurala blushed with embarassment. Even Quintron returned to his senses and shut up.

"AAla-dar, you haven't told us why you came to Rigel?" she asked in a serious manner.

"I brought your sister Luminara here," he answered.

"Luminara. . . That name almost sounds familiar. I have no memories of having a sister. What is she like?"

"Beautiful beyond compare. . . radiant. . . pure, glowing. . ." and then seeing the concern upon Kurala's face, "she's an Angel from the Celestial Realms who has never descended into matter. They probably all look that beautiful. Luminara's your sister, that's what you must have looked like before you were brought to Galaxitron," he explained gently.

"Why did she come here and where is she now?" Kurala asked, visibly softening up.

AAla-dar explained what had transpired between Luminara and Zeon the previous evening.

"You mean that Kurala's sister is on a journey to the Source *beyond* the OMNI?" Quintron asked with astonishment. "That's far out!"

"Will she ever return, AAla-dar? Will I ever get to meet her?" Kurala asked.

"That I don't know. Even Luminara didn't know the answer to that question before she left," AAla-dar answered.

"Now I understand why Zeon said that the power of the OMNI had been breached," she said. Silently thinking to herself, Kurala realized that since Zeon was the bearer of the sphere of light, he couldn't have refused Luminara's request if it had come from a Higher Authority. "Do you know what authority Luminara invoked?" she asked.

"Yes, she said she came by Supreme Command of the Council of the Elohim," replied AAla-dar.

And that's where Lord Metatron resides. He's the one in charge of the circles of light, Kurala realized with mounting excitement. She wished that she could be alone with AAla-dar for there was much that she wanted to share with him. But Quintron must not find out the truth, for he might misuse the information for his own selfish purposes.

Footsteps were heard climbing up the stairway outside. Inside the room, they extinguished the lights and froze into silence. In the dark AAla-dar put his arms around Kurala and held her tightly.

"It's me, Lormax. Unlock the door!"

Quintron opened the door so that Lord Lormax could enter. Turning on the lights, Quintron questioned the Dark Lord. "What happened in the Council?"

"Well, it was pretty wild. Most of the Lords are quite upset over Zeon's murder. He was the best leader the OMNI ever had. Triax and Narcron have never been very popular. They thought that they could build a case against Zeon for treason and finally win everyone's respect, but the opposite has happened. So then we had a secret vote to fill the vacancy within the OMNI. You won't believe who won!" Lormax exclaimed.

"Who did win? I hope that it was you or one of your allies," Kurala asked.

"No, it wasn't any of us, I guess that the Lords wanted a real change. Anyway, to make a long story short, one of you was elected the new member of the OMNI." Lord Lormax looked as surprised as they did.

"What do you mean, one of us?" asked AAla-dar incredulously.

"One of you now belongs to the Triad of the OMNI.

So we've got to return you to the Council. Are you ready to go, Commander Quintron?" Lormax asked.

"Me? Me a part of the OMNI, you've got to be kidding! One minute I'm a prisoner and the next, they want me to be one of their leaders," Quintron grumbled. Kurala could tell that he was secretly flattered.

Unable to suppress a warm smile, she crossed to Quintron and placed her hands on both his shoulders. "Well, Commander Quintron, duty calls. You better go before they come after you. Besides, I bet you're going to be really good at this; you'll make a great OMNI. Maybe you can slip in some good deeds once in awhile and make your mark on history. Seriously, I mean it."

Quintron shrugged in embarrassment. This guy actually had a shy streak which was finally being expressed.

Kurala continued on in a voice filled with inspiration. "You're a good man Quintron, pretty wild and unruly for sure, but you have a good heart. I've always known that about you. And even though you can be rather mean and heartless sometimes, I trust your inherent integrity. I trust you even though you've betrayed me in a pretty big way. Remember, once you're in that position of power that it also brings responsibility with it, especially since you have Narcron and Triax to deal with. But you do have a sense of honor inside you, so allow your honor to express itself. It's so needed here." Kurala leaned forward and kissed Quintron on the mouth. "I forgive you Quintron for everything in the past. Now go forth and be a great Dark Lord!"

Deeply touched, Quintron gave Kurala a quick embrace. "Thanks baby. I'll remember what you said." He waved good-bye to AAla-dar and was gone.

Alone at last, Kurala and AAla-dar sat together on a couch and simply looked at each other. Both of them had changed tremendously since they had last been together on Mebsuta. That felt like aeons ago! The long drawn out war had aged them considerably, but the results weren't so bad. They were wiser and more experienced than before, caring little about the trivialities of life. A new level of depth had emerged from the core of their beings giving them a transcendent glow.

Being reunited gave them much comfort; it really didn't matter that they were currently prisoners of the Dark Lords on Rigel. They could have been anywhere, for their beings had already begun to be anchored in the state of No-Time. The dramas of duality were no longer enticing. All that they wanted to do was to live out the remainder of their allotted span in incarnation as One.

"You realize that now our fate lies in Quintron's hands," AAla-dar commented wryly.

"That's right, so it does. I wonder what he'll choose to do with us?" Kurala mused. "This might be our last time alone together."

"No, it won't be. Even if we are separated or killed, we shall always be together, Kurala," he replied.

"You're right. I guess that this is an eternal kind of love. It just survives and outlasts everything else," she said lightly. "Why are we both so happy when we're in a situation of serious danger?"

"Because it doesn't matter anymore. Nothing matters except that which is timeless, and the love we share is beyond the boundaries of time," AAla-dar said.

"So we're free, no matter where we find ourselves. Separate or together, we are always united in sacred union. . ." Kurala brought AAla-dar's mouth to hers and kissed him playfully. "Like that!"

AAla-dar held her close and kissed her some more. "And like this!"

Δ

Chapter Thirty Five:
THE ASSIGNMENT

That night while they lay sleeping in their beloved's arms, there was a loud knocking at the door. AAla-dar arose and listened carefully to see who it might be.

"OPEN UP!" a voice demanded.

"Who's there?" he whispered.

"It's Exon and Pemmex. We've come on orders from Quintron to bring you to the Council."

"How do we know that this isn't a trick?" AAla-dar asked. Kurala had joined him at the door, looking at him lovingly.

"Look, we don't have time for games. Either you open the door or we will blast it open," the voice replied.

AAla-dar opened the door to admit two of the Dark Lords which he hadn't seen before.

"We brought you some robes. Here, put these on right away. Let's get going!" Exon and Pemmex ushered a surprised, but unresisting AAla-dar and Kurala from their brief respite.

Δ Δ Δ

They were taken by bullet car through the streets of Ra-Matah back to the Council of Dark. Removing their dark robes, Kurala and AAla-dar were escorted into the

Council Chambers.

What a different scene awaited them there! The Council was actually quite orderly. Discussion was taking place with an excess of politeness and respect. Dark Lords were raising their hands before they spoke and listening attentively to the others.

AAla-dar and Kurala were seated together where Kurala had sat before. Looking up, she noticed that Quintron was presiding over the meeting with true authority. Amazingly enough, he appeared to be having a great time; he'd even cleaned up his appearance and looked quite distinguished. To Quintron's left, in a position of honor, was Lord Lormax. Triax and Narcron were nowhere to be seen. Finally the matter at hand was resolved and everyone turned their attention to the two new arrivals.

Quintron glanced at Kurala as if he had never seen her before. "Ah, Kurala, welcome to the Council of the Dark Lords of Orion," and acknowledging AAla-dar, he continued, "Greetings to you, Commander AAla-dar of the Confederation." Both Kurala and AAla-dar nodded their heads in reply, while watching Quintron carefully.

"We've invited you to join with us, since you are an important part of our plans for the future," said Quintron with a smile. "We've been reshuffling the OMNI around, sort of updating it you might say. May I introduce you to our newest member, Lord Lormax? Sorry to say, but Triax and Narcron aren't around any more. They received a death sentence earlier today which was carried out immediately."

Kurala and AAla-dar listened with bemusement. Quintron had certainly been busy since they saw him last.

"Now we *were* hoping to give you back your ships and crews so you could make a speedy departure. Please believe me, *but that was my plan,*" Quintron

EL AN RA

emphasized this part. "However, the Council has decided otherwise and we need to share their decision with you." Quintron's eyes pierced into Kurala with a burning intensity as if he wanted her to listen beyond what his words were saying.

Quintron continued, "The problem is that we still have a vacancy on the OMNI. When the Council voted on it today they decided on Lord Lormax and one other. They decided that you Kurala, should be the new member of the Triad." Quintron's eyes begged her for forgiveness.

Kurala instantly closed her eyes, trying to shut out the words she had just heard. It was worse than a death sentence. She would never be allowed to leave Rigel or to be with AAla-dar. There was no way the Dark Lords would let her go once she had been chosen.

"And what about Commander AAla-dar?" Kurala asked with withering authority while glaring at Quintron.

"He will be permitted to leave as will the crew of your Galaxitron ship," Quintron replied, still silently begging for her forgiveness.

"May I be given some time alone with Commander AAla-dar before I address the Council with my decision?" Kurala asked, knowing that there was no real choice to be made. It was either accept the commission or she, AAla-dar and all of their crews would be killed.

"Permission is readily granted. You are both now excused from the Council. Pemmex will show you to some private quarters. Commander AAla-dar will depart directly from there, so we thank you Commander AAla-dar for your visit and for your service to the OMNI." Quintron was really getting into his role.

Δ   Δ

In the privacy of their room, they sat quietly holding each other. There seemed to be no purpose in getting sad or angry. It was all just like a bad joke that didn't have any apparent resolution other than surrender.

"Isn't it absolutely ironic that now I've remembered who I am, now that I'm not driven by evil anymore, and now that I just want to live a quiet, peaceful life – that's when I get chosen to be one of the OMNI!" Kurala commented dryly.

AAla-dar felt helpless for the first time in his life. He couldn't think of anything to do to free Kurala. He'd even considered remaining in Ra-Matah to be with her, but knew that it wouldn't be allowed. If only they had access to someone with greater wisdom. . .

"Kurala, what about Neptha El Ra? Can you still communicate with her?" he asked.

"I don't know. I haven't contacted Neptha for a long time. Everything got too confusing after Rastaban," she explained. "Why do you mention her now?"

"Because I want you to try to get in touch with her and explain our situation. See if she has any advice for us," AAla-dar replied.

Closing her eyes, Kurala turned her attention to Neptha. Soon the shining image of Neptha appeared before her.

"Greetings Kurala – and AAla-dar is here too, what a wonderful surprise!" said Neptha with rainbow lights and dancing bells.

"Why hello, Neptha, I didn't think that I'd be able to see you," replied an astonished AAla-dar.

"And why not, are we not all from the One?" said Neptha. Then turning her attention to Kurala, "You are doing wonderful work, Kurala. I'm glad that you finally contacted me."

"Neptha, you must be aware of my present situation. What can I do? I don't want to be one of the OMNI. AAla-dar and I want to go off somewhere quiet and live out the rest of our lives together."

"Beloved Kurala, you must accept this assignment to be a member of the OMNI. There is important work to be done and you have the needed combination of energies to fulfill this mission. Remember the circle of light which Zeon carried within him? Well, you will be the one within the OMNI who bears it now. This is essential in order to maintain the proper balance within the template of duality. AAla-dar must depart while he is given the opportunity to go in safety. Send Shakarr and the rest of your crew with him." Neptha paused while noting that Kurala was trembling with sobs. AAla-dar wiped the tears from her face with deep tenderness.

"Will I never see AAla-dar again?" Kurala asked.

"On the contrary, your work together has just begun. Simply have faith and await the appropriate moment. I can't tell you anymore at this time, but call on me whenever you need help." Neptha flashed them a beautiful smile and disappeared.

"What did she mean about our work together just beginning?" Kurala asked. "How can that be, when you have to leave and I have to stay?"

"That I do not know," AAla-dar replied, "but I shall keep watching for an opportunity for us to be together again. Can you tell me more about the sphere of light which Neptha mentioned?"

Since Zeon was dead and she was going to be the next holder of the circle of light, Kurala told AAla-dar everything she knew about it, including how one of the members of his Council of Light contained a circle of dark.

AAla-dar promised to himself to discover who it was the next time that he was called there.

As their conversation finally lapsed into silence both Kurala and AAla-dar knew that the time for their parting was near. She wrote a note for him to give to

Shakarr, explaining why he was to travel with AAla-dar. Then there was their last kiss.

"Again, good-bye," she said.

"Again, good-bye," said he.

Then as she walked out the door, he called after her, "Kurala, remember that we are always free despite whatever responsibilities we have taken on and that the love we share is eternal!"

"Yes, AAla-dar, I will remember!" she replied.

BUT DARE I CRY

It has been a lengthy journey
well washed by years of tears.
Each moment felt to its fullest
until I became that ecstasy,
that deeply etched sorrow,
those well-worn cares,
the fleeting winds of freedom —
as well as the shining pearls
of sacred love shared.

I have seen it all,
tasted its myriad flavors,
and finally in my weary fullness,
I have worn the mantle of its Essence
as no longer separate from me.

My journey is nearly complete.
Having traveled all paths,
now merged into one,
the road is easier to travel.
My load is lighter
as am I.

Although I am still moved
by the murmurs of life
and the soarings of spirit,
I no longer pause

to shed the tears
that I have shed before
and before . . .
and before . . .

For I am homeward bound
and shall not tarry or be waylaid
by that which is already known.
My uncharted voyage is to the Star
beyond the open door,
returning to the Oneness
we have always been.

So, please don't ask me to cry.
My tears have all been shed.
Instead I shall embrace Myself
in all my radiant fullness.
Returning home
by bringing everything inside,
merging stars with body,
becoming ever more Myself,
expanding into limitlessness
within this simple form
until boundaries are erased,
the marriage takes place
and freedom reigns . . .

Chapter Thirty Six:
URIEL-LA'S GIFT

Upon leaving Rigel, AAla-dar set out immediately for Arcturus. The Galaxitron ship belonging to Kurala accompanied him this far. Here he arranged for re-settlement of Kurala's crew except for Shakarr who accepted AAla-dar's invitation to remain with him. AAla-dar had liked Shakarr right away and quickly won his undying loyalty. The old spider was full of tales of Kurala and for the first time, AAla-dar heard the stories of Kurala's capture by the Shamo. This helped him to understand the full breadth of what she had undergone.

He was overcome with a constant, tingling love for Kurala. No, it was more than that – for he felt that they now lived inside each other. He could feel her inhabiting his body, in constant communication with him. Sometimes it drove him wild with desire, for the object of his affections resided within him and how could he make love with himself? But despite his enduring obsession with Kurala, he did his best to carry on, knowing that someday, some way they would be together again.

After delivering a full report to the Intergalactic Confederation Headquarters, AAla-dar was next summoned before the Council of Light. He was accompanied there by the leader of the Confederation. As soon as they arrived in the Council Complex, AAla-dar was asked to make a private visit to Uriel-la.

"Go ahead, AAla-dar, I will await you in the Council," said the Confederation's leader. "While we are waiting for your return, I shall present your report to the Council."

As he approached Uriel-la's personal quarters, AAla-dar wondered at the reason for this visit. Never before had he been invited to a private audience with any members of the Council. At the door to her room the attendant who was guiding him urged him to go inside. So with a soft knock on the door, AAla-dar entered.

He was astonished to discover that Uriel-la was lying in bed, obviously near death. Moving to her side, he gently took her hand.

"Uriel-la, it is AAla-dar. What has happened to you?" he asked with concern.

"Oh AAla-dar, I'm so glad that you have finally come. I've been waiting a long time for you," said Uriel-la in a weakened voice. "I'm dying as you can see, but I've been holding on until you came. There is something of great importance which I must tell you before I go."

"You shouldn't strain yourself talking. Maybe we could just sit in the silence together," said AAla-dar obviously concerned at her condition.

"No, there is little time left for me. Listen carefully to what I'm about to say." Uriel-la then explained to AAla-dar that she was the one within the Council of Light who carried the circle of dark.

"I have just returned from Rigel and I met your counterpart there, the Dark Lord with the circle of light. He was the head of the OMNI." AAla-dar recounted all the details he could remember about Zeon especially noting how handsome he was, knowing that it would give Uriel-la some strength and needed understanding.

When he had finished, Uriel-la had tears in her eyes.

"Thank you AAla-dar, I needed to hear that he truly existed. I've felt his presence for such a very long time. And how was Zeon when you left?" she asked.

"Right before I departed, he was killed by the treachery of the other two members of the OMNI," AAla-dar replied gently.

"Now I understand. How was he killed, by what means?" Uriel-la asked.

"By poisonous laser darts in the back," he replied.

"That's just where my pain began, although now the poison has spread throughout my entire system. I'm dying, because he has died and we are irrevocably linked to each other," she said.

"Maybe you are meant to be together somewhere else, after your bodies die here," AAla-dar commented.

"Yes, that is likely to be so. I can feel us drawing closer together. . ." Uriel-la drifted away for a few moments, then stirred herself back to consciousness. "AAla-dar, I don't have much longer. When I die, you are going to be reassigned to the Council of Light for you are the one chosen to receive my circle of dark."

AAla-dar looked at Uriel-la with mute incomprehension. Surely he didn't hear her correctly. This was all getting too strange. "Excuse me, what did you say?"

"You are chosen to bear the circle of dark within the Council of Light," Uriel-la repeated calmly.

"Please don't ask me to accept another heavy responsibility. Couldn't you choose someone else? Look, I've experienced too much lately what with the war and some personal matters. I'm getting burnt out and what I really need is to go off somewhere alone and be quiet," AAla-dar interjected wearily.

"You are chosen because you have the proper integrity to carry the sphere of dark. You don't really have the right to refuse nor did I long ago, although at first I also tried to resist," she remarked sharply, with a piercing look into his eyes. "Stay with me until I die, it will only be a few minutes longer, then you must go to the Council and take your appointed seat."

Knowing that the matter had already been resolved, even before he had been notified, AAla-dar agreed. "All right Uriel-la, I will take on another responsibility and serve on the Council." He tenderly took her hand, "I am honored to share your time of transition with you."

The woman closed her eyes in relief and turned her attention within so that she could prepare for her impending transition. AAla-dar sat quietly grieving – not so much at the passing of Uriel-la, for that was simply a shifting of consciousness from form to formless, but rather he mourned the final loss of his innocence. Like Kurala, he too had been trapped by responsibility. Their capabilities had placed them in key roles for fulfilling the Higher Purpose of all. And it was true that they no longer had any choice in the matter, for obviously they had made their choices long ago.

With a long slow sigh, Uriel-la took leave of her body. AAla-dar could see her spirit rise out of her physical form. Great wings unfolded as Uriel-la assumed her full Elohim Light Body. She emanated Light like a fountain, showering the entire room with her golden radiance. Assuming a state of vastness, Uriel-la's transparent form grew hundreds of feet tall. With a gracious smile she bowed to AAla-dar, closed her eyes and spiraled upwards in flight to take her seat upon the Council of the Elohim.

Profoundly moved, AAla-dar remained motionless for some time, savoring the memory of Uriel-la's amazing ascension into grace. Then, straightening his shoulders in silent resignation, duty called him to the chambers of the Council of Light.

△△△ △ △△△

Inside the zone of overlap, Metatron stood overlooking the Council of Orion regarding the Council proceedings with a detached concern. Within these horseshoe shaped chambers, the debate raged on with heated emotion. Lords of both Dark and Light questioned whether or not this dimensional universe was ready to graduate from the template of duality. Although the discussions continued night and day for weeks, a consensus could not be reached.

It is important to remember that locked within the template of duality, even the Lords of Light and Dark can become attached to their positions within the conditions of polarity.

Chapter Thirty Seven:
THE EGG

As Luminara aligned with Zeon, their energies fused. Dark and light merged together until only one thing remained. A vibrating circle of light superimposed itself over everything with blinding radiance. Focusing her intent on discovering the Source *beyond* the Dark Lords, Luminara dissolved her being and stepped through the sphere of light.

She found herself alone in a barren landscape of unrelenting greyness. Dead trees which looked like they had been struck by lightning stood out like lonely sentinels against the stark horizon. There was little else to notice except for a moody sky of depressing darkness. The atmosphere was heavy with impending dread.

With a total absence of fear Luminara gazed about, looking for the essence behind this energy patterning. She called forth for the source to reveal itself. Suddenly, an old wizard appeared before her muttering magical incantations. He wasn't at all happy to see her.

"What are you doing here? This is the secret place where all sorcery and magic originate and only the invited may visit. Go away immediately or you will be harmed," he warned in a crackly voice.

"Greetings old wizard!" said Luminara with a smile. "I can see that you aren't real, so don't try to frighten me with your silly tricks."

This didn't please the wizard at all. First of all, he was used to being alone and secondly, on the rare occasions when someone did wander into his realm, they had never challenged the reality of his being.

"Go away whoever you are, you terrible, ugly thing!" he grouched. Bringing out a rusty sword, he made several passes through the air. "Maybe I'll just have to cut off your head!" he threatened.

Luminara smiled sweetly, "You are only a hologram of a wizard; you don't have any substance at all. You don't fool me! Please step aside old phantom projection. I'm on a journey beyond all illusions and I call forth only that which is of the highest Truth!"

As soon as her words were spoken, the wizard and his grey landscape disappeared in an instant. Only bright light remained. Luminara paused and went within to discover what she should do next. When she reopened her eyes, she saw before her a large white translucent egg. This triggered a flickering memory hidden deep inside her . . .

Recognizing the egg to be of utmost sacredness, Luminara shifted her being to her highest state of awareness. Now she was wearing the white, transparent, sparkling dress that she always wore in the Celestial Realms. With a slow, ceremonial dance step, Luminara approached the translucent egg in a sacred manner. When she was around seven feet away she paused and entered the silence for further instructions.

With silent devotion Luminara did her mudra in front of the egg. The light dazzled with shimmering brilliance . . . Time paused as if frozen into the eternal moment . . . For an instant everything ceased to be . . With supreme effort, Luminara returned herself to conscious form. Renewing her resolve she continued on, walking towards the shining egg until she stepped right through it.

Chapter Thirty Eight:
INSIDE

Luminara discovered herself to be inside a small cavern which had a large oval window set into the wall. Through the window she could see numerous stars in a variety of patternings, some of which she recognized, others she did not. It was as if two different universes had superimposed themselves in dimensional overlays, creating a new matrix of inconceivable complexity. What was truly amazing was that this merger of Great Central Sun Systems created one powerful star mandala of striking simplicity!

Glancing downwards, she noticed that a seven pointed star was imbedded in the floor of the cavern. This star was outlined by what appeared to be inset tubes of flowing, liquid violet light. The sound of a low hum resounded throughout the cavern.

As Luminara stepped inside the center of the seven pointed star, a golden beam descended from On High penetrating through her head all the way down into the floor. It is as if she was skewered on the golden beam; it ran all the way down the center point of her being. Then the golden beam activated, beginning to rotate inside Luminara like an internal centrifuge in clockwise manner. She felt herself becoming like a spindle – layers dissolving away as the spinning increased its velocity. As the momentum of the revolutions grew, the golden beam running through her became thinner and finer, as well as surprisingly stronger. In fact, the more delicate it became, the stronger it got.

Luminara spun around like a golden top, losing sight of the cavern. All she could see was the blur of shooting stars, radiating outwards from a central point like fireworks. This central point was far, far away, but in constant direct vertical alignment with her.

She became so vast that her form stretched from one end of the universe to the other.

Reaching the omega point of her spiral, there was a sudden shift as Luminara started to rotate in a counter-clockwise fashion. As she did, she reeled in misty clouds of star firmaments containing myriad nebulas and spiral galaxies. They wrapped around her tightly as she spun inward until she was covered in layers upon layers of soft gauzy starfields. So much has been wrapped around her, that she spins slowly now, laboriously. Luminara is totally hidden by folds of starry firmaments. Throughout this process, the golden beam remains in position in her center, protruding from her head and feet.

All movement ceases . . . Luminara is suspended in space, gently floating upon the starwaves like a cocoon wavering in a breeze, ever anchored on the golden beam.

Part of her yearns to fall asleep, melting eternally into the ocean of timeless bliss . . . Yet she notes that inside her cocooned being, an immense amount of activity is taking place. It feels as if hoards of tiny beings were inside her, everyone engaged in some sort of monumental project.

Looking deeper within, Luminara sees that she is filled with mounds of a straw-like substance which have been honeycombed by tunnels. While she watches, there is a sudden, unexpected conflagration. As the straw ignites, a huge inferno quickly consumes everything.

What remains is hard to describe – soft, curved walls of pinkish membranes with strange shaped nodules and protrusions. There is a long arched corridor extending through the slippery, pinkish membrane walls.

Well aware that she is the whole of what she sees, Luminara is nevertheless called to separate a small portion of herself from the whole in order to explore this arched corridor, knowing with certainty that the corridor leads to an important doorway which must be entered. It is very strange for her to simultaneously experience being both the entirety as well as the small, individualized unit of consciousness able to explore this tiny world more fully. Luminara does not want to sacrifice her beingness of the whole, yet forces herself to focus into this narrow aspect in order to make it through the door.

There it is, a tiny doorway at the end of the corridor. Luminara's fragment steps through. And most wondrously, as she moves through the door, her entire being turns inside out and the whole which she thought that she had to leave behind comes too, along with the fragment!

Δ   Δ   Δ

Here, everything is different, since all has turned itself inside out. It is a silent place – white sand, distant mountains, a still aqua lake in the center. The sky streaked with light in bold strokes. Absolute stillness reigns . . .

Δ   Δ   Δ

Looking closer, Luminara sees that the aqua lake is really an ocean. As she tries to pinpoint herself within this landscape, she realizes that the aqua ocean is the eye of her being.

Silently she asks, "How do I reach the All-Seeing Eye?"

From the heart of silence the answer comes:

TO SEE IS TO BE

TO BE IS TO SEE

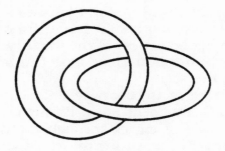

TO ENTER THE TUNNEL

GO WITHIN THE EYE OF THE EYE

   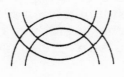

You are within the tunnel.
Spiraling inwards to eye of the eye.
It is spinning, rotating at a 90' angle
inside the larger eye.
It is the seed of an atom.

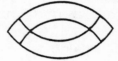 

INTO THE CENTER OF THE FOUR

ROTATING FREELY

INSIDE PYRAMIDS OF LIGHT

ENTERING EYE OF EYE

Difficult to enter since moving so fast.
Slide in on the golden beam
which runs through the center.
Stretch yourself out long and thin.
Rest in the stillness of the center
while ever spinning on the cosmic beam.

Balanced by the four flashing
crystal pyramids of liquid light.
Each pyramid is a diamond transmitter/receiver
emitting pulses of starry frequencies,
codes which regulate crystalline grid matrices.
Spinning double pyramids, backwards and forwards.

In spite of all the movement,
the golden beam in the center of the eye
holds everything in perfect balance.
Og-Min oversee this mandala
as well as all aspects of the golden beam.

SPIRALS TRAVEL

TO EYE ALL SEEING

In the center of inner eye
spiraling smaller and smaller,
becoming a sub-microscopic pinpoint of Light
so small and insignificant, becoming nothing.
Nothingness opens up
into soothing realms of deepest space.
Quiet, profoundly quiet . . .

At first it appears as if no movement exists.
Then you notice that,
like the rising/falling of the starry ocean's tides,
there is a breath,
a steady, constant, deep rhythmic breath.
Slowly, the nothingness breathes in and out.

It is the breath of All That Is
breathing in the perfection of Divine Order.
The great central bellows of God
giving life to everything.
The Divine breathes without thought,
without intent, without effort.
The precision of its repetition is spontaneous,
springing from the eternal heartbeat of the One.

This heartbeat is fueled by Love's Pure Essence . . .
Essence in the state of simply being itself
creates Love.
It is Love . . .

Love is found not only within all of Creation,
it is the glue which binds everything together.
It is both the Seen and the Unseen,
the manifest and unmanifest.
It is the One . . .

You are now beginning to see with the All-Seeing Eye.

Δ   Δ   Δ

Calmly Luminara opens her eye and sees. She has reached the All-Seeing Eye of AN.

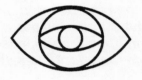

ENTRANCE PLACE

TIMELESS ZONE

OF ALL BEING

ZERO IS ONE

ONE IS ALL

NOTHING IS

Eyes align with Eye.
A heartbeat fades
Into a muted hush.
Star filled space
E X P A N D S.

A sense of knowing,
A deep memory
REAWAKENS.
Instant revelation
In the glorious dawning.

All things open
To see and be seen.
Petals of a flower
Surrendering
Into sun's embrace.

EL AN RA

I can look through
But not yet enter,
Yearning to swim
In the depths
Of timeless ocean.

We are wholes
Within the Whole,
Drops within
The One Drop.
Separation dissolves . . .

Reunion of union
In the world
Beyond worlds.
Everything I see
Within me.

11:11 is a pre-encoded trigger
placed into our cellular memory banks
prior to our descent into matter
under a time-release mechanization,
which, when activated,
signifies that our time of completion is near.

The 11:11 is hereby activated . . .

Chapter Thirty Nine:
THE COUNCIL OF ORION

The chosen messenger was Neptha El Ra. It was she, following the instructions of Lord Metatron and the Council of the Elohim, who sent forth the Call which activated the awakening. This trigger was received by everyone within the vast dimensional universe. It was felt deeply as it embedded into their pre-encoded cellular memory banks. A veil to remembrance was removed. As the memories began to stir and reawaken, an awareness was birthed from the collective unconscious.

Although still somewhat stunned by the enormous sufferings of the intergalactic war which had just been brought to a conclusion, beings everywhere began to see with different eyes. It was as if their glasses had finally been removed. Little by little, clear vision was restored.

With this Great Awakening came the return of a small thread of the music. This Divine melody infused itself into all aspects of life, into all creatures evolved or unevolved. The music began to throb back into consciousness creating a harmonic resonance which could not be denied. This resonance further served the task of remembrance, for it was the entrance of the Song of One.

The 11:11 had hereby been activated. After that,

nothing remained the same. Throughout the myriad corners of this dimensional universe, beings everywhere began to rise up into full remembrance.

The veils of illusion truly dissolved. It was as if a vast stirring was felt in every heart which touched upon a long forgotten memory – a yearning to remember, a yearning to return.

Slowly, one by one, beings everywhere prepared to journey to the vast Council of Orion as if propelled by an unseen force.

The Council itself ever expanded to encompass the many new arrivals to its chambers. The chambers themselves grew organically, almost imperceptibly, to accommodate the ever larger crowds. And each new arrival took their appointed, (dare we say pre-ordained) position on either the side of the light or the dark.

In the middle stood Lord Metatron himself, resplendent in his royal robes and starry crown. By his side was Neptha El Ra now dressed in shimmering white, both of them glowing with the Light of the One.

Each newcomer was greeted with waves of all-encompassing love and they sat down in the full knowing that they had come to the right place – that here their destiny would soon come to its appointed conclusion. They were each imbued with a sense of heightened appropriateness never before experienced to such a degree.

AAla-dar had arrived and sat on the right hand side with the other members of the Council of Light. He too, was filled with a rising sense of expectancy although he knew not the scope of what was to be revealed. But everyone was aware that this was the first time that the entire Council of Light had left their temples on Betelgeuse and traveled together as One to the Council of Orion; thus it's import was clear.

Now there was an outbreak of whispering amongst

221

the assembled Council as the entire Council of Dark Lords from Rigel entered the chambers and were ushered to their seats on the left hand side of the horseshoe shaped chambers. Kurala was here, walking with her head held high. She had never been more beautiful. Her entire being emanated a new radiant purity giving her an almost transparent glow. She had become a true embodiment of the merger of light and dark. Everyone stared at her with open amazement. By her side was Commander Quintron, now called Lord Quintron, closely followed by Lord Lormax.

Once she was seated, Kurala turned to scan the faces of the Lords of Light seated opposite her until she found the eyes of the one she was seeking. A tear began its slow descent down her face as she and AAla-dar gazed at one another again. Finally lowering her eyes, she sat lost in silent contemplation of the immeasurable distance that still separated them. Hearing her name quietly spoken, Kurala looked up to see Neptha El Ra standing before her. Neptha's Presence was flooded in swirling beams of Golden Light, her brilliance impossible to describe in mere words.

Standing to greet Neptha, Kurala felt herself embraced in Golden Light.

"I have a surprise for you, Kurala," Neptha spoke in her musical tones of rainbow light. "Actually, there are two surprises, but the second one you shall receive a little later. Here is the first one."

Neptha stood aside to reveal dear Commander Kowtron standing behind her with a big, shy grin on his face. His soft cow eyes were full of tears of gratitude.

"Oh Kowtron, it's you! How did you get here? I'm so happy to see you! Neptha, how did you ever find him?" Kurala asked with total astonishment.

"It wasn't that easy to locate him for he had gone quite far away," Neptha softly explained. "But once I found all the particles of Kowtron, it wasn't that difficult to bring him back to life, for I am one of the Master Healers, you know."

Kurala embraced Kowtron with great tenderness, then gently released him so that he could go to Quintron who was deeply moved to see his friend again.

Gesturing to Kurala to follow her, Neptha led her out of the Council into a small ante-room. Once they were alone, Neptha turned quite serious.

"Kurala, I must ask you for a great favor. There is one thing that must take place here today before we can go any further. There must be a symbolic union between dark and light. We must have a wedding ceremony. And you have been chosen to be the bride."

As the meaning of Neptha's words sunk in, Kurala's face darkened with pain and there was a sudden flash of her old tempestuousness. "Oh wonderful, I've been *chosen* again. Why can't they choose someone else for a change? Haven't I been chosen enough? Chosen to be captured from the Celestial Realms, chosen to be married to a spider king, chosen to start the most devastating war in intergalactic memory, chosen to be appointed a member of the OMNI! I'm sorry Neptha, but *being chosen* doesn't have very pleasant connotations to me."

Throughout Kurala's outburst, Neptha listened with patience and quiet compassion. "Kurala, you know that everything serves the Higher Purpose," she answered calmly.

"Well, maybe it serves the Higher Purpose, but possibly the Higher Purpose doesn't serve me!" Kurala retorted. Then softening a bit, she said, "Neptha, I'm sorry for complaining, but isn't there some point we reach where we have simply given enough? Surely there must be someone else who can get married this time?" she asked with a quiet desperation.

"No, it must be you," Neptha replied with simple authority.

"Then who am I to marry this time, maybe a snake or a fish?" Kurala said wryly, feeling a profound sense of weariness descend upon her.

"It's a man from the Council of Light, but his identity cannot be revealed to you until after the ceremony is complete. This is a *symbolic union*, meaning that through your wedding all elements of dark and light are married together in sacred union. Therefore there must be no element of personality involved in the marriage ceremony itself. It must simply be the pure union of dark and light signifying the completion of duality. That's why someone of your stature is needed, why you have been chosen. Will you undertake this last mission in order to set all of us free?" Neptha implored.

Nodding her head in joyless ascent, Kurala agreed yet one more time to be chosen as an instrument for the fulfillment of the Divine Plan.

Orion ...
Now that I know your secret
I have no more fear.

Your pockets of darkness
have no hold over me.
My shame,
my guilt have all been released.

By interlocking your pyramids
of duality
within me
I am set free ...

Chapter Forty:
UNION

Powerful music of inspiring majesty filled the chambers of the Council of Orion as Kurala was led forth wearing her flowing dark robes. Her head was entirely covered by a heavy black veil which nevertheless sparkled as though sprinkled with myriad tiny stars. Ahead of her, she could barely make out the tall figure of a man dressed in robes of white, whose face was also covered by a thick veil.

They were led into position facing each other. Beside them stood both Lord Metatron and Neptha El Ra.

Metatron spoke:

"We have been gathered here to celebrate a sacred union between light and dark, a union never before possible within this dimensional universe. This union signifies the completion of the template of duality as well as the entrance into a New Octave of mastery, freedom and Oneness."

Turning to the couple beside him, he asked, "Do you both vow to serve the One with the fullness of your Presence?"

"I do," answered the woman in black with her total commitment, for truly what else remained for her to serve.

"I do," answered the man in white. His voice radiated strength and courage.

Neptha held forth a crystal chalice filled with a bubbling Golden Elixir. "Now as a sign of your commitment to merge light and dark into the Great Light of Oneness, please drink deeply of the nectar of your full surrender to your inherent Oneness. And as you do, all barriers to separation will dissolve. You shall forever be One."

Upon hearing Neptha's words, Kurala wavered for a moment. Fighting back tears, for she didn't even know who she was joining in Oneness with, she quickly strengthened her resolve and focused on her Essence, setting her personality aside as she remembered that this was a symbolic union. She must simply be the essence of dark unifying with the essence of light. With absolute clarity she knew that if duality could be unified and completed there would be no more wars, no more suffering or injustice, no more pain of separation.

As the crystal chalice was handed to her, she brought it to her lips underneath her veil and drank deeply, feeling the Golden Elixir warm her entire being with all-encompassing love. Her weariness slipped away forevermore as she was filled with great tenderness. Lovingly, she handed the chalice to the man standing before her and watched as he too, drank deeply of the elixir of love.

As the sacred union moved to its completion, the celestial music rose into a magnificent crescendo of the most loving sounds she had ever heard, then slowly faded into a gentle glimmer of purest love. The sky above them filled with beams of white light.

Then most delicately, the Angel Luminara descended into the center of the Council, spiraling down a light beam on her beautiful wings of Light. Only a reverent hush of total awe could now be heard.

Beyond the veils
of time and space
there is ever
only One.

Remember
and be released
from the realms
of light and dark.

The Song of One
resonates
across the Celestial Vastness
dissolving
the illusion of separation
forevermore . . .

The True Essence of Being
emerges
as a Star is reborn.

There is only
the Light of the One
shining
in perfect, radiant simplicity.

All-encompassing Love
penetrates all
birthing us
into the New Octave.

Surrender your dreams
into the Greater Reality
that we may fully awaken.

Chapter Forty One:
LUMINARA

And thus Luminara spoke to the assembled Council of Orion:

"Beloved Ones of the One:
I have just returned from a journey never before attempted.
I have seen things never before seen,
for I have looked into the Unseen.
I have traveled through the Eye of AN
into the realms of the Invisible.

And although my entire being
has called me to remain in that Essence
which could not before be seen or even perceived
by those residing within this dimensional universe,
I have returned to you . . .

I have returned to you bearing a great gift
which I humbly offer to each one of you.
This gift is the key to your completion.
It is the map to Beyond the Beyond.
It contains the doorway to your impending freedom.
Inherent in this doorway is the safe passage through this corridor
into realms of Light and octaves of Love previously unimagined.

The Invisible has been penetrated.
Iridescence now floods into not only these Council
chambers,
but into this entire dimensional universe of duality
for the very first time.
This is made possible by my return
to the fields of form.

Imbedded irrevocably into the very core of my being
is the template of Oneness.
As I stand here amongst you
the reign of duality begins to weaken and dissolve.
The veils of the illusion of separation melt away
forevermore . . .

The limitations of time, space and matter
that have long held back the true expression
of your natural state of being
have loosened their hold.
You are hereby released from the shackles of
duality.
You are finally free to fully Be.

I bring to you the gift of the endless expanse of
No-Time,
the forever now.
I stand before you,
anchoring my being into the Greater Reality
that all of you may finally experience and know with
total certainty
both what truly is, as well as what is not.

And I call you forth to come with me
as we journey home to our One Radiant Star of Love.
To do this, we must join together as One,
surrendering all our layers of myriad disguises

until we stand naked in the Light of our purest Presence.

And then, there shall only be One."

Luminara paused and gazed intently at the assembled multitude. She waited for their response . .

Kurala stepped forward without hesitation and said: "I am ready to fully surrender my dark robes for I know that I am neither light nor dark. Long ago, I have merged them into One." She removes her dark robes and her veil. As she does, a stunning radiance begins to flood her being, clothing her in her true form of Light. There is a murmur of appreciation from the Council.

Next AAla-dar comes forth: "I willingly prepare myself to journey into the Unknown, for now that I have united with my Beloved, there is nothing within duality to hold me back." As he removes his robes from the Council of Light, AAla-dar's entire being fills with a glowing splendor.

Gasping with surprise, Kurala finally realizes who she has just married. "AAla-Dar, it's you whom I have wedded!" she says with joyous astonishment.

"How could it ever be anyone else?" he replies tenderly, for he had recognized her immediately. "Fulfilling our Divine Missions is not always painful and arduous, you know." AAla-dar's eyes sparkle at Kurala with loving reassurance as he takes her hand. A blinding beam of Light surrounds the two of them that have become One.

Suddenly another voice speaks up forcefully. It is the gruff voice of Commander Quintron, now choked with emotion. "Here's my robe. I never did like belonging to any side anyway. I guess that some of us loners were just holding out to be All One instead of alone." Shrugging off his robe, Quintron lights up like the other two as his Light Body is activated.

A clamor rises throughout the Council of Orion. In close succession, Shakarr, Kowtron, Lormax and many others throw off their robes and step into their true bodies of Light. Soon everyone was removing their robes of duality. The Council of Orion had become exceedingly bright!

Looking at Neptha and Metatron, Kurala noted that they were already clothed in the Light of the One. It simply hadn't been visible to the others before.

Luminara stood silently in the center of the Council of Orion in her full radiant Presence with wings outstretched. Slowly she began to do her mudra and as she did, the clamor within the Council faded away. A vast quiet descended upon them, covering them like a blanket of feathers – so soft and deep had the silence become. All present drank deeply from the hushed essence of true peace.

Moving to her sister, Luminara embraced Kurala. As Kurala gazed into the clear, shining eyes of her sister, the floodgates to her memories began to open. She finally knew with complete certainty that she was an Angel, remembering what it was like to fly freely throughout the vast, starry heavens.

"Oh Luminara, at last! Thank you, it's been so long," Kurala said in total awe. Turning to her husband she whispered, "AAla-dar, I remember now!"

He could see the dramatic transformation within her as new levels of her being rose to the surface after being long suppressed.

Falling to her knees before her sister, Kurala murmured gratefully, "Thank you beloved sister. Thank you for watching over me for so long and for finally returning me to myself."

"Your wings have returned too, dear one," Luminara replied with a sweet smile. "But they shall appear only when you need them. Everyone here has them, for they are part of our Light Bodies. And your Star Commander played a large part in your reawakening too, you know."

"Yes, I know that. It was a combination of you, AAladar, Neptha & Vega wafers that did it. And beloved Shakarr, of course," she said to the ancient spider who hobbled up next to her, quite beside himself with joy.

Gently came the sound of Celestial singing, growing ever closer. Golden, White Light descended upon the hushed assemblage.

Then a most unexpected thing happened. For the very first time since the inception of duality, the circular shaped Council of the Elohim appeared in the sky above them. As the singing became louder still, heralding the arrival of the Hosts of Heaven, the Council of the Elohim slowly spiraled downwards, gently rotating into position until it was fully docked into the center of the Council of Orion.

Lord Metatron raised his arms in greeting.

"It is done. The template of duality has been completed. Now you are ready to go forth as One. My task is complete. Our Divine Missions have been fulfilled. As we move through the great Doorway of the 11:11 Luminara shall go first leading the way, for she has created the passage which is the channel for our mass ascension. I shall remain here until the very end, for my task is to close the doorway behind us."

Luminara rose into the air above the Council, bowing deeply to the Elohim and the assembled Light Beings.

"Beloved Ones of the One: This shall hereafter be known as my Last Discourse. For soon, there shall be no more to say. Words will no longer be necessary. Already they have become an encumbrance, for in the heart of silence as expressed in the language of Light, infinitely more can be conveyed."

"We are gathered together to journey forth as One. In order to make this journey we must all be prepared to let go of all that we have known and experienced within this dimensional universe. We must willingly release our attachments to all previous personal identities. We must simply stand in the pure, direct beam of the Beloved Star of our Unified Presence and be the perfect embodiments of that which we truly are and that which we *always* have been."

"The great cosmic play of duality is finally over. Now as we lovingly discard our costumes, we shall begin to remember what the drama was really about. Your passage through duality has served us all. By returning to full remembrance, by our joining together as One, we have transformed our Star, moving it to an ever Higher Octave of Alignment with a yet Greater Central Sun System. The Higher Purpose is hereby brought to completion. You are graduating into mastery and freedom – into the long sought after wholeness. You are going Home . . . And as you return to conscious Oneness, the Star itself becomes ever brighter."

"As we pass through the open doorway before us, the template of duality shall be turned inside out, freeing all of you who have chosen Oneness over separation, who have chosen the Greater Reality over the illusion of limitation."

"In the sphere of duality, the highest attainment which you could achieve as an individualized unit of consciousness was the state termed *Unconditional Love.* Now we shall leave even that behind, as we move into the realm of *All-Encompassing Love,* where love simply is – all pervading, inside outside, everywhere. It is the glue which holds our Star together. Where there is no more 'I love you,' for we are no longer living under the illusion of separation, but where love – simply is . . . It is the foundation of everything."

"Form and matter as you have known them are undergoing a tremendous transformation. They are no longer separate from spirit. Heaven has truly merged with Earth as has dark with light. And neither form nor matter shall be the primary focus of where we base our reality, for they are no longer our predominant reality."

"As we move into the realms of the Invisible, we journey into the subtle realms – Octaves of Light so radiant and pure, vastly powerful, yet delicately sweet. That which was previously invisible will become the major portion of what we see and experience. We shall begin to extend our beings into the infinite expanse of the All That Is, finally discovering how vast and unlimited we truly are."

"As we become ever larger, merging our individual consciousnesses back into the pool of shared Essence, all that was anchored into form shall become increasingly smaller and smaller until we simply forget that it ever was. By anchoring our beings in the vast sea of Oneness, duality merges forever into the One. Your Mission within the template of duality is complete. The door to deliverance is open."

"Now as you prepare yourselves for your journey through the doorway of the 11:11 into the New Octave, you are ready to receive your gift. I have brought this gift to you from the other side of the doorway. Please close your eyes and turn inwards as I irradiate you with the iridescent energies from the New Octave . . ."

Luminara gracefully moved her arms in a sacred mudra. Subtle strands of fine iridescent Light flowed forth from her being, bathing the entire Council with soft beams of iridescence, irradiating them from On High.

The entire Council
melted into
the Light of the One.

Time stopped forever
as all moved into
an enduring state of No-Time.

Very gently,
the doorway
between
the two spirals of evolution
opened up.

Without a sound,
duality
turned itself inside out
and ceased to exist.

One by one as One,
the assembled multitude
began to move forward
through the doorway
into the exquisite realms
of the Invisible . . .

Simultaneously,
the Unseen
moved forward
into the Council chambers.

The transfer was in position . . .

The iridescent doorway
into the Invisible
was fully open . . .

Thus began the Council of One . . .

ACKNOWLEDGEMENTS:

Once again it is time for me to offer my heartfelt, deepest gratitude to the many who aided, inspired, encouraged and prodded me to write this book.

Especially:
Grace (Lumiere Amurai) – for traveling the entire distance with me.

The Starry Star-Borne Staff:
Aarela, Alarielle, Azuria, Elara Zacandra, Paloma, Saanwyn & Zeram – for your dedication, commitment, support and laughter!

Nova – for the courage to be yourself.
Nion – for sharing me with so many.

Sorali, Sunyar & Diamona, *intrepid explorers of the Unknown* – for journeying with me through realms of Light.

Tara & the Tauhara Centre in New Zealand – for the refuge of silence wherein I could complete this book.

Elariul (Erik Berglund) – for being such a shining example of service beyond self.

Makua & Reta Anra, Solaihim, Solamé, Mika-Alla, Helios Corona, Aqliaqua, Savanti Ra, Zolanda, Solar, Sumenka, Solani, Kortron & Solinus, Matisha, Siolana, Muana Illumina, Kumari, Am Thrall, Shalomar & Alairius.

To the Orion beings on Earth who are still playing out their roles as Lords of Dark and Lords of Light – thank you for helping to set me free.

And most specially – to the multitudes of Angels incarnate, the Star-Borne who are remembering that we are One and preparing for the homeward journey.

AVAILABLE FROM STAR-BORNE

BOOKS BY SOLARA

EL*AN*RA:
The Healing of Orion
A timeless romance set during the intergalactic wars leading to the completion of duality. $14.95

The Star-Borne:
A Remembrance for the Awakened Ones
A vast handbook of remembrance, highly recommended for all Star-Borne Ones. $14.95

The Legend of Altazar:
A Fragment of the True History of Planet Earth
A profoundly moving story of Atlantis, Lemuria & Beyond, which triggers the core of remembrance. $12.95

Invoking Your Celestial Guardians
Learn how to contact & embody your Golden Solar Angel. This beloved book transforms lives. $6.95

AUDIO CASSETTES BY SOLARA

THE CELESTIAL MESSAGE SERIES
Guided meditations by Solara with music by Etherium
Part 1: **The Angel You Truly Are**
Contact your Golden Solar Angel and find your Starry name. $10.00
Part 2: **The Star That We Are**
Unseal the Akashic Records, send Divine Intervention and remember, release & fly! $10.00

Part 3: **Remembering Your Story**
Remember your own Divine Origins and Mission$10.00
Part 4: **Star Alignments**
A powerful process to anchor in your Light Body.$10.00

STAR-BORNE INITIATION SERIES
*Excerpts from the Star-Borne narrated by Solara
with original music by Etherium.*
Archangel Mikael Empowerment
Side 1: A powerful initiation to reclaim your Divine
Heritage.
Side 2: Archangel Mikael's stirring anthem $11.00
Voyage on the Celestial Barge
Side 1: A healing Voyage of Remembrance
Side 2: Music of the Celestial Seas $11.00

OTHER STAR-BORNE PUBLICATIONS

A Language of Light – Grace
A book of exquisite poetry written by an Angel who speaks
to the heart of Essence $10.00
Love All the Way – Matisha (Cassette)
Heart filled songs for the homeward journey $10.00

Our newsletter, **The Starry Messenger**, is available for
yearly subscription at $25 – US, $30 – Canada, $40 – Foreign

Star-Borne Unlimited
2005 Commonwealth Drive
Charlottesville, VA 22901

US FUNDS ONLY
(Please add $3.50 shipping for first item,
50¢ for each addt'l item.)

271